# THE
# WORLD'S
# FASTEST
# AIRCRAFT

Patrick Stephens Limited, part of Thorsons, a division of the Collins Publishing Group, has published authoritative, quality books for enthusiasts for more than twenty years. During that time the company has established a reputation as one of the world's leading publishers of books on aviation, maritime, military, model-making, motor cycling, motoring, motor racing, railway and railway modelling subjects. Readers or authors with suggestions for books they would like to see published are invited to write to: The Editorial Director, Patrick Stephens Limited, Thorsons Publishing Group, Wellingborough, Northants, NN8 2RQ.

# THE
# WORLD'S
# FASTEST
# AIRCRAFT

## MARTIN W. BOWMAN

From SuperMarine S6 to the Space
Shuttle

Patrick Stephens Limited

First published in 1990


British Library Cataloguing in Publication Data

Bowman, Martin W., 1952-
  The world's fastest aircraft.
  1. Aircraft
  I. Title
  629.133

  ISBN 1-85260-093-4

Patrick Stephens Limited is part of the Thorsons
Publishing Group, Wellingborough,
Northamptonshire NN8 2RQ, England.

Typeset by Burns & Smith, Derby
Printed in Great Britain by Bath Press, Bath, Avon

10  9  8  7  6  5  4  3  2  1

# CONTENTS

# THE QUEST FOR SPEED

The first controlled and sustained power-driven flight took place near Kill Devil Hills, Kitty Hawk, North Carolina, USA on 17 December 1903 when Orville Wright flew the 12 horesepower chain-driven 'Flyer' at an airspeed of 30-35 mph (48-56 km/h) and an altitude of 8-12 feet (2.43-3.65 m) for twelve seconds, watched by his brother Wilbur and five coastguards.

Thereafter there was no stopping man in his quest for faster and further flight. The first officially recognized flight in the British Isles was by Samuel F. Cody, an American, who flew 1,390 feet at Farnborough on 16 October 1908. The following year Louis Blèriot flew the English Channel from Les Baraques in his native France to a meadow near Dover Castle.

The first Gordon Bennett aeroplane race took place on 29 October 1910, at Belmont Park, New York, and Claude Graham-White covered the 62 mile course to win in a 100 hp Gnome-Blèriot in one hour one minute. A Blèriot piloted by Lieutenant de Vaisseau Conneau won the circuit of Europe and Daily Mail Circuit of Britain races in June-July 1911. The following June T.O.M. Sopwith, again in a Blèriot, won the Daily Mail First Aerial Derby, covering a course of some 81 miles at an average speed of 85.5 mph (137 km/h) in 1 hour, 23 minutes.

In 1912 French armaments industrialist Jacques Schneider declared a trophy for seaplane races. However, only two Schneider Trophy Races took place in Europe before the continent was plunged into a Great War. On 16 April 1913 Maurice Prèvost, a Frenchman appropriately, was the contest's first winner, in Monaco, flying a Deperdussin fitted with a 160 hp Gnome at a speed of 73.63 mph (118 km/h). The race was again held in Monaco the following year, when Howard Pixton won the trophy for Britain in a Sopwith Schneider at a speed of 139.66 mph (224 km/h).

The First World War, 1914-18, interrupted speed and record breaking attempts generally but aeronautical and aircraft engine design developed in leaps and bounds as the Allies and the German air arms improved their designs in the race for aerial supremacy. With the signing of the Armistice record breaking resumed. One of the aircraft used in the conflict, a DH 4A, piloted by Captain F.L. Barnard, won the first Kings Cup Air Race on 8/9 September 1922 by covering the Croydon-Glasgow-Croydon course in 6 hours, 32 minutes at an average speed of 123.6 mph (199 km/h).

Meanwhile, others had set the crossing of the Atlantic as their goal. On 16 May 1919 Lieutenant Commander Albert C. Read and his five-man crew set off in an NC-4 Curtiss flying boat of the US Navy to make the first crossing of the Atlantic. They took off from Newfoundland and landed in Lisbon, Portugal, on 27 May after stopping off en route in the Azores.

Captain John Alcock and Lieutenant Arthur Whitten Brown made the first non-stop transatlantic flight, from St John's, Newfoundland to Clifden, County Galway, on 14/15 June 1919 in a modified Vickers Vimy, stripped of all its military equipment and carrying 865 imperial gallons of fuel instead of the normal 516 gallons. It completed the 1,890 mile journey in 16 hours, 27 minutes. On 26 May 1961 a Convair B-58 Hustler completed the New York to Paris transatlantic flight in 3 hours 19 minutes.

The third Schneider Trophy Race took place in 1919 at Bournemouth. Although it was won by Guido Janello of Italy in a Savoia S 13 with a top speed of 109.77 mph, the contest was later declared null and void. Italy won the next two races, held in Venice in 1920 and 1921, and Britain edged in front in 1922 when a Supermarine Sea Lion II designed by R.J. Mitchell and piloted by Henri Biard won with a top

speed of 145.70 mph (234 km/h).

America won the trophy for the first time in 1923 at Cowes with a US Navy sponsored team. The Curtiss engines were too much for their European competitors, who withdrew from the 1924 contest. In October 1925 the contest was held in Baltimore and the all-conquering Americans, led by Lieutenant James Doolittle in a Curtiss R3C-2, raised the speed to 232.57 mph (374 km/h). Three days after the contest, in the same aircraft, Doolittle set a world speed record for seaplanes at an average speed of 247.17 mph (298 km/h).

Italy won the 1926 contest before British in-genuity in the shape of the Supermarine S 5/S 6 series of high-speed streamlined floatplanes stamped their authority on the races. Britain was the outright winner of the Schneider Trophy with three successive victories in 1927, 1929 and 1931 (no contest was held in 1928 and there was no British entry in 1930). The Super-marine S 6B was the first aircraft in the world to exceed 400 mph (644 km/h) and its designer, R.J. Mitchell, later embodied all that was best in the sleek racer in his prototype Spitfire. The Rolls-Royce V-12 engine that developed almost 2,000 hp was another British success

**Above** *Jimmy Doolittle stands proudly on the float of the Curtiss R3C-2 seaplane in which he won the 1925 Schneider Trophy Contest. (USAF)*

**Above right** *Italian Macchi M67 has an early morning engine run on the slipway in front of Calshot Castle during the 1929 Schneider Trophy Contest. Both M67s dropped out of the contest with engine problems. (via Derek N. James)*

**Right** *Macchi MC72. Although not ready in time for the 1931 Schneider contest, in 1934 Agello set a new world speed record of 440.69 mph (709.07 km/h) in an MC72. (via Derek N. James)*

story to emerge from the contest.

The defeated Italians had some measure of satisfaction in 1933 when Francesco Agello recaptured the world's air speed record by at-taining 423.8 mph (682 km/h) at Lake Garda, Italy, in a Macchi MC 72 seaplane. Five MC 72s were built but two crashed on test flights. They had not been ready in time for the 1931 Schneider contest because of engine develop-ment problems. The terrific torque generated by the power of the massive Fiat AS 6 engine (two 12-cylinder AS 5s mounted in tandem) drove the aircraft round in circles on the water and prevented it from taking off. This problem was eventually solved by using contra-rotating propellers. In 1934 Agello set a new world

speed record of 440.69 mph (709.07 km/h) in the MC 72.

While the world's air speed records were held by racing seaplanes from 1927 to 1939 some excellent civilian landplanes were also produced. On 3 September 1932 Jimmy Doolittle set a new landplane record of 296.287 mph (477 km/h) in the barrel-shaped Gee Bee R-1 Super Sportster during the Cleveland National Air Races. Pilots had to compete around a closed-course aerial racetrack with towering multi-coloured pylons at each turn. The racers were 'home built' and very difficult to fly, with the pilot having to sit in a cockpit on or very near the tail assembly to balance the massive engine in the nose. The Gee Bees were named after the five Granville Brothers of Springfield, Massachusetts. All seven Gee Bees built, including two Super Sportsters, which came to grief in 1933, were written off in crashes. Salvageable parts from both the R 1 and R 2 were combined in a new aircraft for the 1935 Bendix race but this aircraft also crashed.

In 1933 Jimmy Wedell in a Wedell-Williams set a new record of 304.5 mph (490 km/h) at Glenview, Illinois. In 1934 the French recaptured the landplane record when Raymond Delmotte set a speed of 314.3 mph (506 km/h) in a Caudron C 460 at Istres, France. The enigmatic multi-millionaire Howard Hughes got into the act a year later, flying his own design, the Hughes H-1, which was among the first to be constructed almost entirely of aluminium. Hughes set a new record of 352.4 mph (567 km/h) at Santa Ana, California.

In Europe the most notable contest for landplanes between the wars was the MacRobertson Race of 20–23 October 1934. This contest involved a hazardous 11,333 miles from England to Australia and was won by one of three de Havilland DH 88s entered for the race. 'Grosvenor House', piloted by Scott and Black, completed the distance in 70 hours, 54 minutes at an average speed of 158.9 mph. Geoffrey de Havilland later developed the DH 88 design to help create the Mosquito fighter-bomber of the Second World War.

In Germany the Nazi Party was anxious to promote superiority in their new aircraft designs even if truth had to come second to propaganda. In 1937 a factory-built Messerschmitt Bf 109E was extensively modified for an attempt on the world air speed record. Hermann Wurster, Messerschmitt's chief test pilot, set a new landplane record of 379.6 mph (611 km/h) and after-the-flight photographs taken by the Nazis showed it to be a 'production Bf 109.' On 30 March 1939 Flugkapitän Hans Dieterle set a new landplane record of 463.9 mph (746.45 km/h) in a highly streamlined Heinkel He-100V but the world was led to believe that the feat had been achieved in an He113 production model.

On 26 April 1939, Flugkapitän Fritz Wendel established a world speed record of 469 mph (755 km/h) in a Messerschmitt 209 although for propaganda purposes it was described as the Bf 109R or racing version of the standard production fighter. Even so, the speed was not bettered by any other propeller-driven aircraft for thirty years. In 1941 an Italian Fiat CR 42B fitted with a 1,010 hp Daimler Benz DB601A engine, became the fastest recorded biplane with a top speed of 323 mph (520 km/h).

German and British designers had long turned their attentions to jet power and as early as 1937, Frank (later Sir Frank) Whittle had run the first gas turbine aero-engine in Britain. On 27 August 1939 Germany won the race when the Heinkel He 178 became the first jet aircraft to fly. The Heinkel He 280 became the world's first twin-engined jet fighter when it flew on 5 April 1941 but it did not enter production. The first jet aircraft to enter operational service was the Messerschmitt Me 262, which made its initial flight in April 1941, powered by a single Jumo 210G piston engine mounted on the nose. It was not until July 1942 that the third prototype was flown with Jumo 004-0 jet engines. By D-Day 1944 about thirty Me 262s had been delivered to the Luftwaffe but none were operational until 3 October 1944.

Meanwhile, in Britain, on 15 May 1941

**Above** *Gloster E 28/39 W4041 which made its maiden flight at RAF Cranwell on 15 May 1941 powered by a single 860 lb thrust Whittle W 1 turbojet — the first flight by a British jet-propelled aircraft.* (Hawker Siddeley)

**Right** *P-39 Aircomet 44-22633 on display at the only piece of grass in the Mojave Desert at Edwards Air Force Base, California. The P-39 flew before the RAF Meteor.* (Author)

Whittle's engine was used in the first flight by a British jet aircraft, the Gloster E 28/39. That same year, in America, the Bell Aircraft Corporation had been requested to undertake development of a jet fighter design to take advantage of early British design work on gas turbine engines. The Airacomet flew for the first time on 10 October 1942 but never saw action. Britain's first operational jet fighter, the Gloster Meteor I, entered squadron service in July 1944. The first production Meteor Mk I was sent to the USA in February 1944 in exchange for a Bell YP-59 Airacomet as part of an Anglo-American agreement reached in mid-1943.

By 1945 Britain had gained a world lead in jet fighter design which was not seriously chal-lenged by America until 1947. Early American jet aircraft had not proved successful. The first American jet bomber design was the Douglas XB-43, which first flew on 17 May 1946. It had a maximum speed of 507 mph (816 km/h) and a crew of three but did not enter production. On 7 November 1945 a British Meteor F 4 of the High Speed Flight established a new world air speed record of 606 mph (975 km/h). On 7 September 1946 Britain increased the record to 616 mph (991 km/h).

It was June 1947 before America captured the record, with the Lockheed P-80R Shooting Star, which raised the record to 623.74 mph (1,003.60 km/h). The Douglas Skystreak raised it even further that year to 650.92 mph (1047.33 km/h). The F-86 Sabre, America's

first supersonic jet fighter, reigned supreme from 1948–1953. This swept-wing fighter was one of several immediate post-war aircraft to benefit from German wartime research into jet and rocket engine development and wing design.

The first British supersonic flight was made on 9 September 1948 by John Derry in the de Havilland DH 108 during a dive. (Derry was killed on 6 September 1952 at the 13th Farnborough Airshow when his prototype DH 110 broke up in mid-air during a dive in an attempt to produce a sonic boom). Also in 1952, Convair produced the XF2Y-1 Sea Dart in response to a US Navy project for a waterborne jet fighter. The Sea Dart had no hull. Instead, take-off and landing was performed on extendable hydro-skis. Three examples were flown, with one fatal accident. The Sea Dart remains the only waterborne aircraft to have flown faster than the speed of sound.

It was not until September 1953 that Britain, with the Hawker Hunter 3, recaptured the

**Above** *The Douglas XB-43 was the first American jet bomber design and had a maximum speed of 507 mph (816 km/h). (McDonnell Douglas)*

**Above right** *The first prototype DH 110 WG236 in which John Derry first exceeded the speed of sound on 9 September 1948 during a dive. (de Havilland)*

**Right** *Canadair-built Sabre and a Hawker Hunter both of No 112 Squadron, RAF. These two record-breaking aircraft closely contested the world air speed record in the early 1950s. (MoD)*

world air speed record and in September 1953 the Supermarine Swift 4 increased it to 735.70 mph (1183.74 km/h). The Douglas F4D-I Skyray enjoyed a brief claim to fame when Lieutenant Commander James B. Verdin, USN, eclipsed this within a month with a speed of 752.94 mph (1,211.48 km/h). The record stood for 25 days. In October Lieutenant Colonel Frank Everest, USAF, set a record of 755 mph (1,215 km/h) in an F-100 Super Sabre. In August 1955 Colonel Harold Hanes, USAF, set the first supersonic air speed record, also in

an F-100. The FAI (Féderation Aèronautique Internationale) ruled that the record could now be set at any altitude and not just at sea level.

America went on to all but dominate high-speed flight. Exceptions were the Fairey Delta, which set a new record of 1,132 mph (1,821.39 km/h) in March 1956, and the Soviet-built Sukhoi Type E-66, with which Colonel Georgiy Mosolov achieved a record speed of 1,483.83 mph (2,387.48 km/h) in October 1959. The same pilot set a new world air speed record of 1,665.9 mph (2,681 km/h) in an E-166 in 1962.

On 14 October 1947 America had made the first manned supersonic flight when Major Charles 'Chuck' Yeager was air-launched from a B-29 bomber in the rocket-powered Bell X-1. Although the X-1 repeatedly exceeded the world's speed record of 616 mph (991 km/h) the speeds were never officially recognized because international regulations did not include air-launched flights. Twenty years later the North American X-15A-2 attained Mach 6.72 after being air lifted to altitude by a Boeing B-52. On 23 August 1963 the X-15A-2 reached

**Above** *Hawker Hunter 3 WB188 which set a new world air speed record on 7 September 1953. (Hawker)*

**Right** *Lockheed C-140 Jetstar. On 22 April 1962 Miss Jacqueline Cochrane set no less than 29 World Point-to-Point records, including Washington to London, in a Jetstar. (Lockheed)*

a height of 354,200 feet (107.98 m).

Meanwhile, Britain continued to develop its lead in commercial jet design. In May 1952 the de Havilland DH 106 Comet I was the world's first pure-jet airliner to enter airline service when BOAC used a Comet I on the London-Johannesburg route. The first supersonic airliner in the world was the Tupolev Tu-144, which flew for the first time on 5 June 1968. It achieved supersonic speed for the first time on 5 June 1969. In 1977 it began a weekly passenger service within the Soviet Union but scheduled operations were terminated within just seven months.

The BAC-Sud Aviation Concorde, whose French prototype flew for the first time on 2 March 1969, followed by the first British aircraft on 9 April 1969, has proved eminently

more successful. On 21 January 1976 Concorde became the first supersonic airliner used on passenger services and on 1 January 1983 a British Airways Concorde set a New York–London passenger record of 2 hours, 56 minutes.

At the other end of the scale, air-racing using propeller driven aircraft is still a major participation sport even in these supersonic times. One of the most notable civil racers used in class racing is the 230 mph (370 km/h) Cassutt Racer, which was designed and built by Captain Tom Cassutt, an American airline pilot, in 1954. In it he won the 1958 US Formula One Championship and in 1959 he produced the slightly smaller Cassutt Special II. Many Cassutts, including some built under licence in the UK by Airmark Ltd, are still flying today. Another notable survivor is a single Miles Hawk Speed 6, one of three built in the mid-1930s and which came second in the 1949

King's Cup Air Race. In 1965 Ron Paine, the pilot, was awarded the SBAC Trophy outright having logged the fastest time in King's Cup races in 1958-59 and 1962-64.

The fastest racing machines are the warbirds of the 'Unlimited' Class. Every year warbirds such as the P-40, Mustang, Spitfire and Corsair F4U-7 — all in private hands — compete in air races throughout Europe and the USA. It is a tradition that has grown since the war. In 1947 F4U Corsairs were placed first and second in the Thompson trophy event at the Cleveland

*The F4U-1 Corsair Navy fighter of WWII set a number of post-war speed records in the Cleveland Air Races in the USA. (Vought)*

Air Races, breaking the closed course record with an average speed of 396.13 mph (638 km/h). In 1949 Corsairs were placed 1-2-3 in the event.

Surplus RCAF P-51 Mustangs, of which over 200 were made available in the early 1960s, are among the most popular 'Unlimited' Class racers. These and other warbirds regularly surpass speeds of 430 mph (692 km/h) and draw crowds of 100,000-plus at the annual Reno Air Races in Nevada, USA. In 1966 a privately owned Hawker Sea Fury set a world air-speed record for piston engined aircraft of 520 mph (836 km/h) in Texas. The FAI accredited record for a piston engined aircraft is 517 mph (832 km/h) by Frank Taylor in a modified North American P-51D Mustang over Mohave, California, on 30 July 1983. In 1979 Steve Hinton reached a speed of 499.1 mph (803 km/h) in his Griffon-engined, twin-propeller, RB-51 Mustang at Tonopah, Nevada. This aircraft was destroyed soon after during the Reno Air Races.

Two of the most notable events in Britain are the Cranfield Grand Prix and Formula One Race. This type of racing has evolved from the American pre-war sport of Pylon Racing and in Britain first gained prominence after a design competition to produce a Formula One Racer in 1963. Pilots race anti-clockwise round a hexagonal course approximately three miles long, with their turns marked by aluminium pylons 25 feet high. Europe's largest closed circuit air race is the Digital Schneider Trophy Race, which in 1984 was revived in modern form from the series of contests competed for by seaplanes from 1913 to 1931. Today, the con-

*Two of the fastest 'Unlimited' Class thoroughbreds are the Bearcat (foreground) and the Hawker Sea Fury (background), which in 1966 set a world piston-engined record of 520 mph (836 km/h). (Author)*

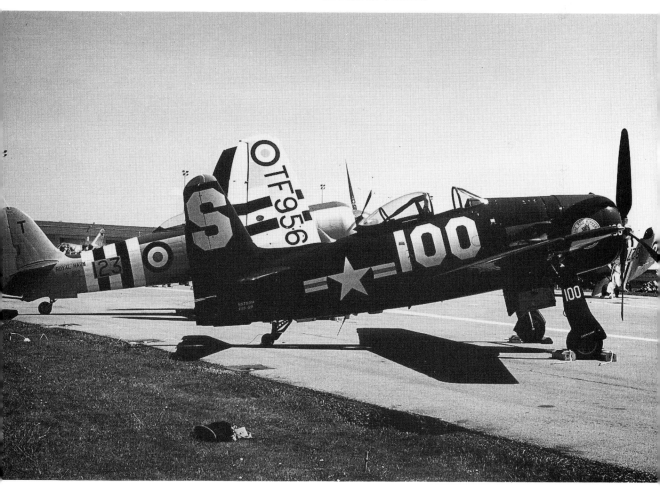

test is a handicapped air race for piston engined land aircraft up to 12,500 lb (5,681 kg) in weight. The most powerful aircraft in the 1987 race.was a Curtiss P-40 Kittyhawk piloted by Ray Hanna, who was disqualified but who averaged 257 mph (413 km/h) in the heats.

The Soviet Union has the distinction of currently having both the fastest propeller driven and fastest combat jet in the world. The Tu-114 turboprop transport aircraft is capable of 545 mph (877 km/h) and the Mikoyan MiG-25 is currently the fastest combat jet in the world with a top speed of Mach 3.2 (2,110 mph) (3,395 km/h). However, America takes

*Many of over 200 Surplus RCAF P-51 Mustangs like this one were bought in the early 1960s for the popular sport of 'Unlimited' Class racing. The FAI accredited record for a piston-engined aircraft is held by Frank Taylor in a modified North American P-51D Mustang over Mohave, California, on 30 July 1983. (Canadair)*

top billing with the SR-71A, which still holds the air speed record of 2,193.167 mph (3,529 km/h) set in 1976, while the fastest aircraft of all time is the NASA/Rockwell Space Shuttle Orbiter 'Columbia' which in 1981 broke all records for space by a fixed wing craft with a speed of 16,600 mph (26,715 km/h).

# AEROSPATIALE- BAC CONCORDE

**Type**: *Supersonic airliner* **Crew**: *Three* **Manufacturers**: *BAC, Filton, Bristol and Aerospatiale, Toulouse* **Power Plant**: *Four 38,050 lb st (17,259 kg) Rolls-Royce/SNECMA Olympus 593 Mk 602 afterburning turbojets* **Dimensions**: *Span, 83 ft 10 ins (25.56 m); length, 202 ft 3½ ins (61.66 m); Height, 37 ft 1 in (11.30 m)* **Weight**: *Empty, 174,750 lb (79,265 kg); Loaded, 400,000 lb (181,435 kg)* **Performance**: *Max cruising speed, 1,354 mph (2,179 km/h) at 51,300 ft (15,635 m) or Mach 2.05*

On 29 November 1962 the British and French Governments signed an agreement to provide development funding for a supersonic airliner while four companies — British Aircraft Corporation, Rolls-Royce, Sud-Aviation and Sociètè Nationale d'Etude et de Construction de Moteurs d'Aviation — agreed to collaborate on airframe and engine design and production. It was decided that the cruising speed would be no more than 1,400 mph (2,254 km/h) at

*Concorde comes in to land with droop snoot lowered.* (Author)

63,000 feet (19,207 m) to allow the aircraft to be built of aluminium alloys, which would be cheaper than stainless steel, or titanium, which would have been needed to withstand the higher temperatures at speeds above Mach 2.2.

Several research aircraft were built to aid development of a new supersonic airliner. The BAC 221 was modified from the airframe of the Fairey Delta FD 2 to flight test the delta-wing planform and the Handley Page HP 115 slim-delta aircraft was designed to investigate the lower end of the speed range.

Prototype Concorde construction began in February 1965 and the new project soon caught the imagination of several of the world's major airlines. By 1971 sixteen major airlines took out options for a total of 74 Concordes but today only Air France and British Airways operate a Concorde fleet. The high cost of development was a big factor. It proved too large an obstacle for the Boeing 2707 project of 1967–71 and the only other contender, the Soviet built Tu-144, which flew for the first time on 31 December 1968, was never adopted for regular passenger services.

The first French Concorde prototype flew on 2 March 1969 at Toulouse and the second British prototype on 9 April 1969. Concorde

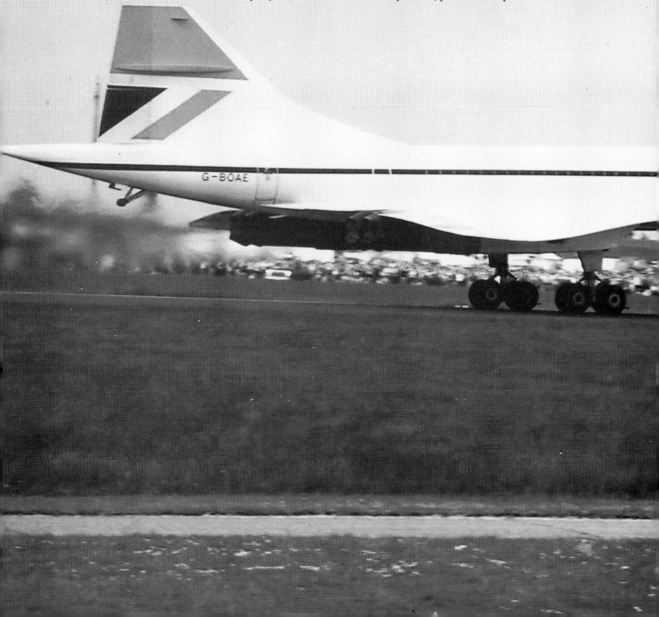

first exceeded Mach 1 on 1 October 1969 and Mach 2 was passed during a test flight on 4 November 1970. The first of two pre-production aircraft flew on 17 December 1971 and the first production example on 6 December 1973.

On 21 January 1976 British Airways and Air France began simultaneous passenger flights between London~Bahrain and Paris~Rio de Janeiro respectively. The inaugural flight to the USA was made on 24 May 1976 when two Concordes, one each from Air France and British Airways, landed at Dulles Airport, Washington DC. After months of legal wrangling services began between London~New York and Paris~New York on 22 November 1977. The New York~London record for Concorde is 2 hours, 56 minutes, 35 seconds, established on 1 January 1983.

A total of 16 production Concordes was built by April 1979. Five are currently operated by British Airways and four by Air France. The Concorde can carry 128 passengers over a distance of 3,915 miles (6,304 km).

*British Airways' Concorde cutting a dash during the 1984 Mildenhall Air Fete. (Author)*

# CONVAIR B-58 HUSTLER

**Type**: *Supersonic medium bomber* **Crew**: *three* **Manufacturers**: *Convair Division of General Motors, Fort Worth, Texas* **Power Plant**: *Four 15,600 lb st (7,090 kg) (with afterburner) General Electric J79-GE-3B turbojets* **Dimensions**: *Span, 56 ft 10 in (17.10 m); Length, 96 ft 9 in (29.54 m); Height, 31 ft 5 in (9.6 m)* **Weights**: *Loaded, 160,000 lb+ (72,727 kg)* **Performance**: *Max speed, 1,385 mph (2,230 km/h) at 40,000 ft (12,195 m); Service ceiling, 60,000 ft (18,292 m)* **Armament**: *One General Electric T-171E3 Vulcan 29 mm cannon in radar-aimed tail mounting. Four wing mounted pylons for a variety of weapons and a mission pod under aircraft centreline to carry nuclear or conventional bomb loads*

*Convair B-58 Hustler 55-0661, second of the first 13 test aircraft seen here with its disposable fuel and weapons pod. (Convair)*

The B-58A was the first supersonic bomber to enter production for the USAF and the winner of no less than 19 speed and altitude records.

Original Convair design studies for a manned supersonic bomber began in 1949 and in January 1951 the company submitted a proposed design to the USAF. In August 1952 a contract was placed for 13 test aircraft, with 17 more to follow later.

The first B-58 left the Fort Worth assembly building on 31 August 1956. A feature of the B-58 (Convair Model 4) was its droppable centreline pod which carried a portion of the aircraft's fuel supply and its nuclear payload. From late 1963 a number of Hustlers were equipped with a dual pod with fuel in the lower compartment and an optional photo-reconnaissance capability in the lower compartment.

The Hustler's heat resistant skin and delta wing were constructed of fibreglass, aluminium and stainless steel honeycomb sandwiched be-

tween two layers of metal. Miniaturization was employed where practical and many automatic systems made the task of operation and monitoring easier for the crew. The B-58 was the first aircraft from the outset to be built around a weapons system concept.

The B-58A flew for the first time on 11 November 1956 and flew supersonic for the first time on 30 December that year. Some 30 trials aircraft were used extensively by Convair and then by a USAF B-58 Test Force at Carswell AFB, Fort Worth, Texas. On 5 June 1957 the first demonstration of a B-58 dropping its disposable pod on a target took place. On 29 June the aircraft made its first Mach 2 flight. On 18 September 1959 it demonstrated low-level capabilities in flight from Fort Worth, Texas, to California, flying at almost 700 mph (1,127 km/h) at a maximum altitude of 500 feet (152 m) above the ground. Every YB-58 and the two XB-58s were fitted with J79-GE-1

turbojets but the twelfth aircraft was re-engined with the J79-GE-5A.

On 1 December 1959 the USAF took delivery of its first production model B-58A at Carswell AFB. On 15 March 1960 Strategic Air Command officially designated the 43rd Bomb Wing at Carswell AFB as the first unit to operate the B-58A. Two weeks later, on 23 March, a US Air Force crew completed the longest B-58 mission thus far, approximately 11,000 miles (17,713 km) at 620 mph (998 km/h) in 18 hours, 10 minutes non-stop with two air-to-air refuellings. In August the 43rd Bomb Wing's Hustlers became operational and that same month SAC accepted its first TB-58 trainer.

By 1961 86 B-58As had been ordered and the 116th and final B-58 (including eight TB-58A trainers) was delivered on 26 October 1962. The only other unit in which the B-58 served was the 305th Bomb Wing, but the aircraft gained world fame with a string of speed and performance records.

On 12 January 1961 two B-58s from the 43rd Bomb Wing based at Carswell AFB, Fort Worth, set three new international speed-and-payload records at Edwards AFB, California. Major Henry Deutschendorf and crew claimed a record speed of 1,061.80 mph (1,709 km/h) over a closed-circuit 2,000 kilometre (1,242 mile) course. This flight also broke records for no payload, 1,000 kilogram payload and 2,000 kilogram payload. Two days later Major Harold E. Confer and crew claimed a record speed of 1,284.73 mph (2,068 km/h) over a 1,000 kilometre course to win the Thompson Trophy. On 10 May 1961 a B-58 flew a closed course at an average speed of 1,302.07 mph (2,096 km/h) for more than 30 minutes to win the Blèriot Trophy.

On 26 May a B-58 piloted by Major William R. Payne established a New York to Paris speed record, covering the distance in 3 hours, 19 minutes, 51 seconds at an average speed of 1,050.25 mph (1,753.06 km/h). For this, the crew won both the MacKay Trophy and the Harmon Trophy.

On 5 March 1962 a B-58 piloted by Robert G. Sowers won both the Bendix Trophy and the MacKay Trophy for non-stop Los Angeles~ New York~Los Angeles flight that set three new records: Los Angeles~New York, 2 hours, 58.71 seconds, average speed of 1,216.47 mph (1,954.79 km/h); New York~Los Angeles 'beat the sun' flight, 2 hours, 15 minutes, 50.8 seconds, average speed of 1,083.42 mph (1,741 km/h) and round trip, 4 hours, 41 minutes, 11.3 seconds, average speed of 1,044.96 mph (1,682 km/h).

On 18 September 1962 the B-58 set two world altitude and payload records with a flight to 85,360.84 feet (26,035 m). On 16 October 1963 B-58s of SAC 305th Bomb Wing made two flights to lay claim to five more world speed records, including the longest supersonic flight in history, from Tokyo to London non-stop (the first aircraft to do so). A B-58A flown by Major S.J. Kubesch made the 8,028 mile (12,927 km) trip in 8 hours, 35 minutes, 20.4 seconds at an average speed of 934.57 mph (1,504.89 km/h). The B-58 finished 1963 as holder of a total of 19 officially recognized world speed and altitude records.

The B-58 was retired from Strategic Air Command on 31 January 1970.

*The B-58A was the first supersonic bomber to enter production for the USAF and winner of no less than 19 speed and altitude records. B-58As first began equipping Strategic Air Command in 1960. (Convair)*

# DASSAULT MIRAGE FAMILY

**Type**: *(III and 5) Interceptor; (IVA/P) Strategic Bomber; (2000) Multi-role combat aircraft; (F 1) All-weather interceptor* **Crew**: *(III and 5) One-two (IV) Two. (2000 and F 1) Pilot only* **Manufacturers**: *Avions Marcel Dassault/Breguet Aviation, widely sub-contracted with some models assembled in Australia, Belgium and Switzerland* **Power Plant**: *(IVA/P) Two SNECMA Atar 9K turbojets* **Dimensions**: *(IVA/P) Span, 38 ft 10½ in (11.85 m); Length, 77 ft 1 in (23.5 m); Height, 17 ft 8½ in (5.4 m)* **Weights**: *Empty, 31,967 lb (14,500 kg); Loaded, 73,800 lb (33,475 kg)* **Performance**: *(IVA/P) Max speed, 1,454 mph (2,340 km/h) at 40,000 ft (13,125 m); Ceiling, 65,620 ft (20,000 m); (2000C) Mach 2.2+; Service ceiling, 59,050 ft (18,000 m)* **Armament**: *(III), (IVA/P) None. Provision for one 60 kiloton bomb or 16,000 lb underwing stores. (2000C) Two 30 mm DEFA 554 cannon and up to 13,890 lb (6,300 kg) of underwing stores*

On 24 October 1958 the Mirage IIIA-01 closely beat the English Electric Lightning P 1B by a month to become the first aircraft outside the USA and the Soviet Union to reach Mach 2 in level flight. It was an ironic twist of fate, for the Mirage I, which was originally developed in 1952 to meet a requirement by the Armée de l'Air for an interceptor fighter, was first fitted with two British Viper turbojets. These engines enabled the Mirage I, which flew on 25 June 1955, to reach Mach 1.15 in a dive before a rocket motor was added to take the speed to Mach 1.3 in level flight. This arrangement was later replaced with a single SNECMA Atar 101G in the Mirage III, which flew for the first time on 17 November 1956. The first production Mirage IIIC flew for the first time on 9 Oc-

*Dassault Mirage III of the South African Air Force.* (SAAF)

tober 1960 and 244 of them were delivered to the Armée de l'Air.

Meanwhile, in 1954 a decision had been taken to provide France with its own nuclear strike deterrent force and Dassault started work on a bomber version of a 1956 company design for a twin-engined night-fighter. In 1957 the design was dramatically modified so that two Pratt & Whitney J57B turbojets could be fitted to carry the new bomber to the eastern-most borders of the Soviet Union.

Finally, two SNECMA Atar 9K turbojets were fitted and the design was scaled down, with in-flight refuelling being selected as a means of completing the nuclear mission. The Mirage IV-001 flew for the first time on 17 June 1959 and was followed by the first production

IVA, which made its maiden flight on 7 December 1963. Deliveries of some 62 Mirage IVs to the Armée de l'Air Commandement des Forces Aèriennes Stratègic took place between 1964 and March 1968. Currently, about 43 Mirage IVs, including 18 IVP bombers which can carry the ASMP nuclear missile, will continue in the strike/reconnaissance role until 1996.

By the late 1970s well over 1,000 Mirage IIIs, including licence-built models in Australia and Switzerland, had been built for several of the world's air forces. The Mirage IIIE ground-attack version first flew on 5 April 1961. In 1965, following requests from Israel for a clear weather ground-attack version of the Mirage, Dassault used the IIIE airframe and power plant to develop the Mirage 5, which flew for the first time on 19 May 1967. Fifty were subsequently bought (but never delivered) for the Heyl Ha'Avir. Israel went on to develop its own improved version of the Mirage as the IAI Kfir while over 500 Mirage 5s, including about 100 partly constructed in Belgium, were delivered to about a dozen of the world's air arms, including the L'Armée de L'Air.

The latest versions of the Mirage are the 2000 multi-purpose aircraft and the F 1, which was developed by Dassault as a private venture replacement for the Mirage III. The Mirage F 1 prototype flew on 23 December 1966 and deliveries of the F 1C all-weather interceptor to the French Air Force began in 1973. By 1986 189 Mirage F 1s had been delivered to the French Air Force and about 480 for export.

The Mirage 2000 flew for the first time on 10 March 1978 and the 2000N two-seat penetration versions on 2 February 1983. A total of 291 Mirage 2000s and 63 Mirage 2000Ns are on order for the Armée de l'Air. The first Mirage 2000 squadron became operational at Dijon in 1984.

**Above left** *Two Mirage F-1CZs of the South African Air Force.* (SAAF)

**Left** *Dassault Mirage IIIC of the Belgian Air Force.* (Dassault)

# DE HAVILLAND DH 88 COMET RACER

**Type:** *Long-range racer* **Crew:** *Two* **Manufacturers:** *de Havilland Aircraft Co, Hatfield* **Power Plant:** *Two 230 hp de Havilland Gipsy Six R (Racing) engines* **Dimensions:** *Span, 44 ft (13.41 m); Length, 29 ft (8.84 m)* **Weight:** *Loaded, 5,320 lb (2,413 kg)* **Performance:** *Max speed, 237 mph (381 km/h); Range, 2,925 miles (4,707 km)*

In January 1934 Britain faced the prospect of not having a suitable entry for the forthcoming Melbourne Centenary Air Race between London and Melbourne. Sir MacPherson Robertson had put up a trophy and prizes totalling £15,000 for the winners. With no British Government funding available the directors of the de Havilland Company decided to design and build their own long-range racing aeroplane and enter it in the speed section of the race, just ten months away.

The de Havilland Company was prepared to share the cost of entry to the race provided enough orders were received. Purchasers were guaranteed a top speed of 200 mph. By the end of February orders for three Comet Racers at a cost of £5,000 each were received. The first order for a Comet Racer was placed by Mr A.O. Edwards, Managing Director of the Grosvenor House Hotel, London, and would be flown by T. Campbell Black and C.W.A. Scott. In May, Amy (née Johnson) and Jim Mollinson announced their entry in a Comet Racer and the third aircraft was entered by the racing driver Bernard Rubin and flown by O. Cathcart Jones and Kenneth Waller.

Building work on three DH 88s took place at Stag Lane day and night amid great secrecy before final assembly and testing at the new factory at Hatfield. The DH 88 was a streamlined low-wing monoplane design with a small frontal area, all of which compensated for the relatively low power of its two Gipsy Six engines. Wooden construction and stressed skin covering not only saved weight but also speeded up production. Later, these techniques were successfully applied to the Albatross and Mosquito. However, the radical nature of the Comet caused a few technical problems, not least of which were the complicated French Ratier variable pitch propellers, which it was hoped would give better take-off performance in hot climates. The thin wing meant that the fuel tanks had to be installed in the fuselage and the undercarriage retracted into the lower part of the engine nacelles.

The first DH 88 was flown from Hatfield by Captain Hubert Broad on 8 September, with just six weeks left to the start of the race. A month later, on 8 October, the first Comet attained 235 mph (378 km/h) at 1,000 feet and 225 mph (362 km/h) at 10,000 feet (3,050 m). On 14 October the aircraft arrived at the start point at Mildenhall, Suffolk. By now all three Comets were painted in distinctive racing colours. Predictably, Rubin's machine was in British racing green, with racing number 19. The Mollinsons' black aircraft was registered G-ACSP and named 'Black Magic' while 'Grosvenor House', racing number 34, was in gleaming red and white and registered G-ACSS. Only 20 of the original 64 entries made the starting line.

The competitors took off from Mildenhall on 20 October 1934, watched by a crowd of 60,000 people. Their route took them by way of five main control points at Baghdad, Allahabad, Singapore, Darwin and Charleville with several intermediate checkpoints in France, Italy, Greece, Asia and Sumatra. The Mollinsons arrived at Baghdad first after flying the 2,530 miles non-stop in 12 hours, 40 minutes. The other two Comets followed and were joined by a Douglas DC2 airliner of KLM piloted by two Dutchmen, Parmentier and Moll, and a Boeing 247D, crewed by Colonel Roscoe Turner and Clyde Pangborn. The Mollinsons retired from the race at Allahabad with piston trouble caused by unsuitable fuel.

Scott and Black pressed on and completed the 11,300 miles to the Flemington Racecourse in Melbourne with an elapsed time of 70 hours,

54 minutes, 18 seconds to win both the speed and handicap race. Scott and Black were awarded the £10,000 speed prize and the £650 gold trophy but as each competitor could win just one prize, the handicap prize went to Parmentier and Moll in the DC2. Turner and Pangborn were third in the Boeing 247D and Jones and Waller's Comet finished fourth (and third in the speed section). On 2 November 1934 they completed the 23,000 mile return trip in a record 13 days, 6 hours, 43 minutes.

In 1935 two more DH 88 Comet Racers were built, the first being F-ANPZ for the French Government, and the second for Cyril Nicholson and named 'Boomerang' for long-distance record breaking flights. Two of the three original Comet Racers later served in Europe and Africa with Belgian, French and Portuguese operators but G-ACSS returned to Britain, narrowly avoided being turned into scrap following a landing accident, and re-named, went on to take part in further air races. In 1938 it fell into deep neglect but was restored in 1943 and took part in the Festival of Britain in 1951. The aircraft was put on display until October 1965 when it was donated to the Shuttleworth Trust. Fully restored to airworthy condition, 'Grosvenor House' returned to Mildenhall for the US Air Fete in May 1987 — fifty-three years after leaving the airfield for the memorable flight to Australia, since when, after another crash-landing, at Hatfield, it is again being rebuilt.

# DE HAVILLAND HORNET

**Type**: *Long-range fighter and medium range carrier-borne strike aircraft* **Crew**: *Pilot only* **Manufacturers**: *de Havilland Aircraft Co, Ltd, Hatfield, Herts* **Power Plant**: *Two 2,030 hp Rolls-Royce Merlin 130/131 or 133/134* **Dimensions**: *Span, 45 ft (13.7 m); Length, 36 ft 8 ins (11.21 m); Height, 14 ft 2 in (4.32 m)* **Weights**: *Empty, 12,880 lb (5,854 kg); Loaded, 20,900 lb (6,371 kg)* **Performance**: *(F 3) Max speed, 472 mph (760 km/h) at 22,000 ft (6,707 m); Service ceiling, 35,000 ft (10,670 m)* **Armament**: *Four 20 mm Hispano cannon in nose and provision for 2,000 lb (909 kg) of bombs or eight 60 lb (27 kg) rocket projectiles beneath wings.*

The fastest twin piston-engined combat aircraft in the world to reach operational service started life as a private venture before the RAF showed an interest in 1943 in using the aircraft for long-range operations against the Japanese.

A prototype was ordered against Specification F 12/43 and when completed, closely resembled the Mosquito before it. The Hornet was powered by a pair of 2,030 hp Merlins, a 130 to port and 131 to starboard, and was of mainly wooden construction although the wing embodied part wood and light alloy materials. Geoffrey de Havilland Jr was at the

**Below** *de Havilland Hornet F 1 PX217, the seventh production model out of a batch of 60 delivered to the RAF. (de Havilland)*

**Right** *Hornet F 3 PX393 of No 64 Squadron. A dorsal fillet was added to the F 3 version and internal tankage was increased from 360 to 540 gallons for long-range operation. (de Havilland)*

**Below right** *VV430, the first of 79 Sea Hornet NF 21s, which from 1949-54 was the FAA's standard carrier-borne night fighter. (de Havilland)*

controls on the first flight on 28 July 1944 when a speed of 485 mph (780 km/h) was reached. The installation of operational equipment and four Hispano cannon in the F Mk I production model reduced the top speed to 472 mph (760 km/h) at 22,000 feet (6,700 m).

Some 60 F Mk Is were built and the first were delivered to the RAF in April 1945, too late for action in the Second World War. Towards the end of the year the Aircraft and Armament Experimental Establishment at Boscombe Down discovered rudder problems during handling trials and as a result the F Mk 3 version entered production fitted with a dorsal fillet at the tail. Wing tankage was also increased for long-range operation.

The F Mk I entered service with No 64 Squadron at Horsham St Faith, near Norwich, in May 1946 and No 19 Squadron was equipped with the type in October of that year. In March 1951 Hornets of Nos 33, 45 and 80 Squadrons, FEAF (Far East Air Force), took part in 'Firedog' anti-terrorist operations in Malaya, where their rocket-strikes were used to great effect in jungle sorties.

On 19 September 1949 a Hornet piloted by A.C.P. Carver set a non-stop Gibraltar to London record for a piston-engined aircraft with an average speed of 436.54 mph (701.49 km/h) in 2 hours, 30 minutes, 31 seconds. In November 1951 a Sea Hornet *N F 21* of No 809 Squadron completed a flight from Gibraltar to Lee-on-Solent non-stop at an average speed of 378 mph (608.69 km/h).

The last of 204 Hornets were built in June 1952. In Fighter Command Hornets were replaced by the Meteor in 1951 and in FEAF by the Vampire in June 1955. A total of 198 Sea Hornet naval versions saw service with the Royal Navy between 1947 and 1954 when they were replaced by the de Havilland Sea Venom.

# DE HAVILLAND DH 106 COMET

**Type**: *Subsonic airliner* **Crew**: *(Civil) Four; (Military) Five* **Manufacturers**: *de Havilland Aircraft Co. Ltd, Hatfield, Herts.* **Power Plant**: *(Comet 1) Four de Havilland Ghost 50 Mk 1 turbojets each developing 4,450 lb st (2,018 kg).* **Dimensions**: *(Comet 1A) Span, 115 ft (35.05 m); Length, 96 ft (29.26 m); height, 28 ft 4¼ in (8.66 m).* **Weights**: *(Comet 1) Loaded, 105,000lb (47,627 kg)* **Performance**: *(Comet 1) Max speed, 490 mph (788 km/h) at 35,000 ft. (10,700 m); Range, 1,750 miles (2,816 km) with 12,000 lb (5,443 kg) payload*

On 15 May 1946, when the tail-less de Havilland DH 108 took to the skies, it was the forerunner to Britain's lead in jet airliner design. The Goblin 4 powered DH 108 was designed to Specification E 18/45 to provide flight experience of the tail-less configuration planned for the DH 106 airliner (which eventually appeared as the Comet).

*Comet 1 G-ANLO of BOAC landing during the 1953 Farnborough Air Show. (John Hosford)*

The DH 108 was among the first aircraft to encounter the effects of compressibility on an airframe in the transonic speed range. Test pilot Geoffrey de Havilland was killed when the second prototype broke up over the Thames Estuary in September 1946. A third prototype was built incorporating several modifications and in 1948 it established a new closed-circuit speed record of 605.23 mph (974 km/h). On 9 September 1948 it became the first British aircraft and the first jet aircraft in the world, to exceed Mach 1 (in a dive between 40,000 ft (12,200 m) and 30,000 ft (9,145 m)).

Meanwhile, prototypes of the DH 106 design had been ordered in May 1946. In the race for the post-war jet airliner it was this design which won through. The aircraft that emerged was fitted with four de Havilland Ghost centrifugal turbojets and its low-wing had 20° of wing sweepback while the tail surfaces were unswept. The Comet, which could carry 24 passengers, flew for the first time on 27 July 1949. On 11 May 1950 a Comet 1, flown by John 'Cats Eyes' Cunningham, established a Cairo–London speed record of 5 hours, 39 minutes with an average speed of 386.46 mph (621.026 km/h).

Much of the aircraft's initial success was underpinned by the faith shown by BOAC (British Overseas Airways Company) which had undertaken to purchase eight Comets as early as 1946. A total of nine Comet 1s (the aircraft could now carry 36 passengers) were eventually ordered by BOAC, which introduced the first scheduled jet passenger service anywhere in the world on 2 May 1952 when a Comet 1 left London for Johannesburg. Although it did not have sufficient range for transatlantic operations, during its first year of service the Comet 1 operated at an average load factor of 80 per cent.

Britain's world lead in commercial jet transport was severely dented and the initiative finally lost when between May 1953 and April

**Above** *Comet C 4 XR397. One of five C 4s delivered to No 216 Squadron at RAF Lyneham in 1962.* (de Havilland)

**Left** *Comet C 2 XK671 'Aquilla' of No 216 Squadron, RAF Air Support Command.* (de Havilland)

1954 three of the nine Comets broke up in mid-air. It was later established that the crashes were caused by metal fatigue of the pressure cabin structure.

On 7 July 1956 the first of ten Comet Series 2 military transport versions of the civil Series 2 was delivered to No 216 Squadron at RAF Lyneham, to make this the world's first jet transport squadron. The Comet Series 2, which first flew on 16 February 1952, differed from the Series 1 in having four Rolls-Royce Avon engines in place of the earlier Ghosts.

The first production Series 2 flew on 27 August 1953. The RAF operated the C 2 until April 1967 and five Comet C 4s from February 1962 to June 1975.

The first of 75 redesigned and 'stretched' Comet 4 versions had emerged in 1957. On 23/24 October that year John Cunningham established a London–Johannesburg record of 12 hours, 59 minutes with an average speed of 434.56 mph (698.309 km/h) in the Comet 4. On 4 October 1958 two BOAC Comet 4s flew the world's first transatlantic jet services for fare-paying passengers but by then Boeing had gained a world lead with the 707. However, the Comet was successfully developed for RAF service as the Nimrod and it will always be remembered for its pioneering work in the development of high-speed commercial jet transport.

# DOUGLAS D-558 SKYSTREAK/ SKYROCKET

**Type**: *Experimental aircraft* **Crew**: *One* **Manufacturers**: *Douglas Aircraft Co.* **Specification (D-558 II) Power Plant**: *One 3,200 lb st (1,451 kg) Westinghouse J34-WE-22 turbojet and one 6,000 lb st (2,722 kg) Reaction Motors XLR-8 bi-fuel rocket motor* **Dimensions**: *Span, 25 ft (7.62 m); Length, 45 ft 3 in (13.79 m); Height, 11½ ft (3.50 m)* **Performance**: *Max speed, Mach 2.01*

Late in 1944 the USAF and NACA (National Advisory Committee for Aeronautics) launched the Bell X-1 and the US Navy began a separate project of its own as part of the overall military high-speed research programme called D-558. Their entry, the straight-winged D-558 'Skystreak', was similar to the X-1 in shape but it was powered not by a rocket engine but by a jet. The Skystreak was designed to take off con-ventionally from runways and although slower, could stay aloft longer than the X-1.

The D-558-I was designed to investigate jet aircraft characteristics at transonic speeds, including stability and control and buffet investigations. The instrumentation used on board to record detailed wing and tail pressures was designed at Langley Research Centre during the 1930s for use on dirigibles. The first flight experiments with vortex generators, which are used to improve flight performance on many of today's commercial jet airliners, were performed on the D-558-I.

Three D-558-I Skystreaks were built and testing took place at Edwards AFB, California. The first Skystreak flew in March 1947 piloted by Douglas test pilot Gene May. In August 1947 US Navy Commander Turner F.

*D-558-II Skyrocket at the moment of release from its P2B-1S (B-29) mother ship. In November 1953 Scott Crossfield became the first man to fly faster than twice the speed of sound after his Skyrocket had been released from a B-29. (McDonnell Douglas)*

**Above** *In August 1953 the third D-558-II with Major Marion Carl at the controls was air-launched from a B-29. (MacDonnell Douglas)*

**Right** *Three D-558-I Skystreaks were built. In August 1947 US Navy Commander Turner F. Caldwell, flying the first D-558, set a world's absolute speed record of 640.7 mph (1030.95 km/h).*

Caldwell, flying the first D-558, set a world's absolute speed record of 640.7 mph (1,030.95 km/h). Five days later Major Marion E. Carl, USMC, used the same D-558 to increase the record to 650.92 mph (1,047.33 km/h). The US Navy project received a setback in May 1948 when the engine in one D-558-I exploded on take-off, killing the NACA test pilot Howard Lilly.

The second D-558-I was stored to provide spare parts for the other D-558 aircraft and three new models, called 'Phase Two' aircraft, with swept wings, were built. Particular attention was given to the problem of 'pitch up', a phenomenon often encountered with swept-wing configured aircraft.

The first D-558-II Skyrocket was powered by a single jet engine and was designed to take off conventionally, fitted with two JATO rockets to boost climb. It was later dropped from the project and modified to an all-rocket version. The second Skyrocket, also designed to take off conventionally, was powered by a jet engine for take-off and climbing to altitude, and the four-chambered rocket motor installed in the extreme tail was for reaching supersonic speeds. The third D-558-II, another jet and rocket combination, was designed to be dropped from a mother plane.

The Skyrocket first flew on 4 February 1948 piloted by Douglas test pilot John Martin. In June 1950 Douglas test pilot Bill Bridgeman made the first of three test air-launches in the third D-558-II. In August 1951 Bridgeman reached a height of 79,000 feet and achieved a top speed of Mach 1.89 during a test flight. In August 1953 the D-558-II with Lieutenant Colonel Marion Carl at the controls was air launched from a B-29 and he reached an altitude of 83,235 feet (25,387 m).

In November 1953, with the Westinghouse turbojet removed and the rocket fuel capacity doubled, NACA pilot Scott Crossfield became the first man to fly faster than twice the speed of sound when he reached Mach 2.01 (1,327 mph) (2,135 km/h) at a height of 65,000 ft (19,800 m) after his Skyrocket had been released from a B-29.

# DOUGLAS F4D-1 SKYRAY

**Type**: *Carrier-borne interceptor* **Crew**: *Pilot only* **Manufacturers**: *Douglas Aircraft Company, El Segundo, California* **Power Plant**: *One Pratt & Whitney 10,500 lb st (4,772 kg) J57-P-8B turbojet or Pratt & Whitney 9,200 lb st (4,181 kg) J57-P-2* **Dimensions**: *Span, 33 ft 6 in (10.24 m); Length, 45 ft 8 in (13.96 m); Height, 13 ft (3.96 m)* **Weights**: *Empty, 16,024 lb (7,283 kg); Loaded, 25,000 lb (11,363 kg)* **Performance**: *Max speed, 690 mph (1,111 km/h) at 36,000 ft (10,975 m); Service ceiling, 55,000 ft (16,768 m).* **Armament**: *Four 20mm cannon. Up to 4,000 lb (1818 kg) of bombs, rockets or other stores on six external points.*

At the end of the Second World War it was realized that the US Navy needed a lightweight jet interceptor for fleet defence to counter the threat posed by the emergence of Soviet high-speed jet bombers. Above all the interceptor had to possess an extremely high rate of climb. It had to be able to reach a height of 40,000 feet (12,200 m) in under five minutes.

On 17 June 1947 the US Navy signed a contract with Douglas, El Segundo, for a design study and engineering data for a delta winged fighter. The Navy's Bureau of Aeronautics, Fighter Branch, had been interested in low-aspect ratio delta wings for a fighter since the publication of captured German data into such a design at the end of the war.

The Douglas design team, led by Ed Heinemann, added the German data to their own findings and the final F4D planform was selected in 1948 when a contract was ordered for two XF4D-1 prototypes. Intended power for the new design was to have been the Westinghouse J40-WE-6 but production difficulties led to the substitution of an interim engine, the Allison J35-A-17. On 23 January 1951, Douglas test pilot Larry Peyton flew the XF4D-1 for the first time, at Muroc, California.

The advanced nature of the Skyray design and problems with the early engine resulted in a protracted flight testing programme over the next two years. In mid-1952 both prototypes were re-engined with the J40-WE-6 but performance proved disappointing. In September 1953 the 11,600 lb thrust XJ40-WE-8B afterburner engine was installed in the first prototype and at last the Skyray achieved its design potential. On 14 September Douglas announced its intention to attempt a new air speed record, which stood at 727.63 mph (1,170.76 km/h) set by the Hawker Hunter. As XF4D-1 testing, in the hands of Douglas pilot Robert Rahn, continued, the Supermarine Swift pushed the record up to 735.70 mph (1,183.74 km/h).

At Salton Sea, California on 3 October 1953, Lieutenant Commander James B. Verdin, USN at the controls of the XF4D-1, set a new world speed record over 3 kilometres (1.86 miles) with an average speed of 1,211.48 km/h (752.94 mph). This record only stood for just one month, although Lieutenant Colonel Frank Everest's new record speed of 757 mph (1,219 km/h) in a YF-100 over the same course was not faster by one per cent as required in the FAI rules. However, the FAI recognized the absolute speed record as the faster average over *either* the 3 km or 15 km straight courses. North American took advantage of this fact and Everest averaged a speed of 755.15 mph (1,215.04 km/h) over the 15 km course at Salton Sea on 29 October. As this was faster than Verdin's average it was recognized as a new absolute speed record. Despite this, Verdin's 3 km record stood until 28 August 1961 when it was eclipsed by the F4H Phantom.

On 16 October 1953 (13 days after Verdin's air speed record over 3 km) Robert Rahn, in the same XF4D-1, set a new air speed record over a 100 kilometre (62.1 miles) closed course with a speed of 1172.47 km/h (728.11 mph). It was finally broken on 25 February 1959 by Gerald Muselli in a Dassault Mirage III who set an average speed of 1763.28 km/h (1,095 mph).

A decision had been taken in March 1953 to

*The Douglas XF4D-1 Skyray in which Lieutenant Commander James B. Verdin, USN, set a new world speed record on 3 October 1953 over 3 kilometres (1.86 miles) at Salton Sea, California. (McDonnell Douglas)*

On 26 May 1958 at Point Mugu, California, Major Edward
N. LeFaivre, USMC, set five official world aircraft climb
records. The highest goal of 15,000 metres (49,212.5 feet) was
reached in 2 minutes, 36.05 seconds. (McDonnell Douglas)

# ENGLISH ELECTRIC LIGHTNING

fit the Pratt & Whitney J-57-P-8B turbojet in
the production model. That year, following sea
trials aboard the USS *Coral Sea* the Skyray was
passed for carrier operations. On 16 April 1956
the Skyray was delivered to Fleet Composite
Squadron Three (VC-3) at Moffett Field,
California. Some 419 F4D-1 Skyrays were built
by the Douglas plants at Torrance and El
Segundo before production ceased in
December 1958. That year the Skyray
established five time-to-climb records, thus
underlining its potential to 'climb like a
homesick angel'.

**Type**: *All-weather interceptor.* **Crew**: *pilot only*
**Manufacturers**: *English Electric Aviation* **Power
Plant**: *Two 15,680 lb (7,112 kg) thrust Rolls-Royce Avon
302 augmented turbojets* **Dimensions**: *Span 34 ft 10 in
(10.6 m); Length 53 ft 3 in (16.25 m); Height 19 ft 7 in
(5.95 m)* **Weights**: *Empty, 28,000 lb (12,700 kg); Loaded, 50,000 lb (22,680 kg)* **Performance**: *Max speed,
1,500 mph (2,415 km/h) at 40,000 ft (12,200 m); Service
ceiling, 60,000+ ft (18,290 m)* **Armament**: *Two Red
Top or Firestreak guided missiles, or two 30 mm Aden
cannon*

The first British aircraft capable of exceeding
Mach 1 in level flight was the Sapphire-

*The Sapphire-powered English Electric P 1A which broke the sound barrier on its first flight on 11 August 1954. (BAe)*

powered English Electric P 1A, designed by W.E.W. 'Teddy' Petter, and which first broke the sound barrier on its first flight on 11 August 1954. In November 1958 the Avon-powered Lightning attained Mach 2 and became the RAF's first single-seat fighter capable of exceeding the speed of sound in level flight.

The first production Lightning F 1 flew for the first time in October 1959 and the type entered RAF service with the Central Fighter Establishment at Coltishall, Norfolk in December that year. In July 1960 No 74 Squadron, also at RAF Coltishall, became the first operational unit to be equipped with the F 1 and the type became the principal air defence fighter in both Fighter (later Strike) Command and RAF Germany.

In 1963 the F 2, with fully variable after-burner, equipped Nos 19 and 92 Squadrons of RAF Fighter Command at Leconfield. Between 1964 and 1968 the major Lightning variant was the F 3, which differed principally from earlier marks in having its two Aden nose cannon deleted and carrying a pair of Red Top missiles in place of the earlier Firestreaks. Provision was also made for two over-wing fuel tanks and the fin and rudder were squared off at the tip. The Lightning T 4 and T 5 are two-seat trainer versions of the F 2 and F 3 respectively.

In 1965 BAC developed a kinked and cam-

bered wing to improve operation at vastly increased weights and reduce subsonic drag and
thus extend the range. This fully developed
version of the Lightning was originally known
as the F Mk 3A but was later designated the
Lightning F Mk 6. Fuel capacity was almost
doubled by the installation of an enlarged ven-
tral fuel tank containing 600 gallons. The F 6
prototype first flew on April 17 1964 and first
equipped No 5 Squadron at Binbrook in November 1965. All Home Defence F 3s were
subsequently retro-fitted to F 6 standard and
later equipped Nos 11, 23, 56, 74 and 111
Squadrons in Fighter (later Strike) Command.

By mid-1967 all Lightnings were capable of
being refuelled in flight. In August that year
the 338th and final Lightning was completed
on the Preston production line. On April 25
1968 five operational and one OCU Lightning
squadrons led the fly-past over Bentley Priory
to mark the disbandment of Fighter Command. From 1974 Lightnings began to be replaced by Phantoms in the Air Defence role. In
1988 the last two Lightning squadrons, Nos 5
and 11 Squadrons of the Binbrook Wing (and
the Lightning Training Flight), were re-
equipped with the Tornado F Mk 2.

**Left** *Rolls-Royce Avon powered XA847, one of three English Electric P 1B prototypes built, and on 25 November 1958 the first British aircraft to fly at Mach 2. (BAe)*

**Right** *Lightning F Mk 3 XR754 subsequently retro-fitted to Mk 6 standard. (BAC)*

**Below** *Lightning F Mk 6 XS919 armed with Red Top missiles and fitted with over-wing ferry tanks and refuelling probe. (BAe)*

# ENGLISH ELECTRIC (BAC) CANBERRA

**Type**: *Light bomber* **Crew**: *Three* **Manufacturers**: *English Electric Aviation, Preston. Sub-contracted by Avro, Handley Page and Short* **Power Plant**: *Two Rolls-Royce Avon 101 turbojets* **Dimensions**: *Span, 63 ft 11½ in (19.5 m); Length, 65 ft 6 in (19.95 m); Height, 15 ft 7 in (4.72 m)* **Weights**: *Empty, 22,000 lb (10,000 kg); Loaded, 46,000 lb (20,909 kg)* **Performance**: *Max speed, 580 mph (933 km/h) at 30,000 ft (9,144 m) Ceiling, 48,000 ft (14,630 m); Range, 805 miles (1,295 km)* **Armament**: *None. Bomb load, 6,000 lb (2,727 kg)*

Designed by W.E.W. 'Teddy' Petter and known originally as the AI, the English Electric Canberra was the first jet bomber to enter service with the RAF. The Canberra ranks as one of the most successful British designs of all time, with export versions to about ten different nations, where rebuilt versions still serve in some instances as tactical bombers.

Because it was unarmed, the Canberra had to rely on speed alone to outpace interceptors. Specification B 3/45 called for a bomb load of 6,000 lb (2,727 kg) and a radius of action of 750 nautical miles. Petter designed an unswept aircraft with a broad, low-aspect ratio wing which allowed for the highest possible cruising altitude and maximum fuel economy. It also bestowed remarkable manoeuvrability.

The prototype flew for the first time at Warton on 13 May 1949 with Wing Commander Roland Beaumont at the controls. The Canberra B 2 flew for the first time on 23 April 1950. The first production aircraft made its maiden flight on 8 October that year and the first unit to be equipped was No 101 Squadron at Binbrook in May 1951.

Altogether, 430 Canberra B 2s were built. One set a transatlantic record in February 1951 when it was flown from the UK to Baltimore, USA, as part of the deal which led to the Martin Company building the Canberra under licence (as the B-57/RB-57). This was a

milestone in British aviation history. Not since the First World War had the USA built a foreign combat design in their own country.

The PR 3 reconnaissance version had a longer fuselage to accommodate additional fuel tanks and first entered service in 1953. On 8/9 October 1953 a Canberra PR 3, flown by Flight-Lieutenant R.L.E. Burton AFC and navigated by Flight-Lieutenant D.H. Gannon DFC, won the speed section of the London-New Zealand Air Race by flying from London Airport to Christchurch, a distance of 12,270 miles (19,758 km), in 23 hours, 51 minutes at an average speed of 514.465 mph (828.29 km/h).

On 4 May 1953 Wing Commander W.F. Gibb DSO, DFC, had raised the world height record to 63,668 ft (19,406 m) in an Olympus-engined Canberra (*WD952*). On 29 August 1955 Gibb went one better in the same aircraft, raising the world record to 65,889 ft (20,083 m). WD952 was used as a flying test-bed for the Olympus, an advanced version of which is now used in Concorde.

In 1955 Canberras took part in 'Operation Firedog', the emergency campaign against terrorists in Malaya, and during October-November 1956 Canberra B 2s from Cyprus and B 6s from both Cyprus and Malta took part in operations against Egypt during the Suez Crisis.

**Above** *Canberra B 2 WD932. On 17 December 1953 B 2 WH699 'Airies IV', flown by G. G. Petty, set a London-Cape Town record of 12 hours, 31 minutes.* (BAe)

**Below** *Canberra PR 3 WE139, flown by Flight-Lieutenant R. L. E. Burton AFC and navigated by Flight-Lieutenant D. H. Gannon DFC, which won the speed section of the London–New Zealand Air Race on 8/9 October 1953 by flying from London Airport to Christchurch in 23 hours, 51 minutes.* (BAe)

The final Canberra bomber variant to serve with the RAF was the B(I)8 two-seat light bomber/intruder, from May 1956 to June 1972, which differed from earlier Canberras in having a completely re-designed front fuselage with a blister-style canopy offset to port for the pilot and provision for a navigator/bomb aimer in the nose. A detachable gun-pack was mounted beneath the rear section of the bomb bay.

Altogether, some 925 Canberras were built in Britain and a further 49 in Australia. Today only No 100 Squadron of RAF Strike Command at Wyton use the Canberra B Mk 2, T Mk 4, E Mk 15 and TT Mk 18 for target facilities.

# EXPERIMENTAL X SERIES (1946~58)

**Type**: *Experimental aircraft* **Crew**: *Pilot only* **Manufacturers**: *(X-1/2, 1A-1D) Bell; (X3) Douglas Aircraft Co; (X-4) Northrop Aircraft Inc; (X-5) Bell Aircraft; (XF-92A) Convair Aircraft Co* **Dimensions**: *(Bell X-1) Span, 28 ft (8.53 m); Length, 31 ft (9.45 m); Height, 10 ft 8 ins (3.25 m)* **Weights**: *4,900 lb (2,227 kg) plus 8,200 lb (3,727 kg) of fuel*

In September 1946 a NACA (National Advisory Committee for Aeronautics) contingent arrived at Edwards AFB set in the desert wastes of southern California to begin testing a series of experimental jet and rocket aircraft. The first of the rocket-powered research aircraft, the Bell X-1 (originally designated the XS-1), was a bullet-shaped aircraft with a flush cockpit with a side entrance and no ejection seat, that was built to investigate the transonic speed range and, if possible, break the 'sound barrier'.

The first of the three X-1s had been glide-tested at Pinecastle AFB, Florida, early in 1946.

The first powered flight of the X-1 was made on 9 December 1946 at Edwards with Chalmers 'Slick' Goodlin, a Bell test pilot, at the controls. On 14 October 1947, with Captain Charles 'Chuck' Yeager USAF as pilot, the aircraft, named 'Glamorous Glennis', after his wife, flew faster than the speed of sound for the first time. Captain Yeager ignited the four-chambered XLR-11 rocket engines after being air launched from under the bomb bay of a B-29 at 21,000 feet. The 6,000 lb (2,722 kg) thrust ethyl alcohol/liquid oxygen burning rockets, built by Chemical Reaction Motors Inc, pushed him up to a speed of 670 mph (1,078 km/h) or Mach 1.015 at a height of 42,000 feet (12,800 m).

Another USAF pilot, Lieutenant Colonel Frank K 'Pete' Everest Jr, was credited with taking the X-1 to its maximum altitude at 71,902 feet in August 1949. Eighteen pilots in all flew

*Major Chuck Yeager, here being congratulated by Larry Bell, was the first man to fly faster than the speed of sound in the X-1. (Bell)*

*Bell X-1A and Bell X-1B pictured near the Muroc Dry lake facility.* (Bell)

the X-1s. 'Queenie', the number three aircraft, which was fitted with a low-pressure fuel system, was destroyed in a fire on the ground while mated to its B-29 mother-ship in November 1951 before ever making any powered flights. Fortunately, the USAF test pilot Joe Cannon, who was in the X-1 at the time, had a lucky escape. He managed to run to safety but was badly burned by leaking fuel and was out of action for almost twelve months.

The X-1A, X-1B and X-1D were growth versions of the X-1. They were almost five feet longer but had an improved rocket propellant system and had a 'combat canopy'. The X-1A and X-1B were modified to have ejection seats.

Their mission was to continue the X-1 studies at higher speeds and altitudes. Despite

its nomenclature, the X-1D was completed before the X-1A and X-1B, and the X-1C was never built (the X-1 was rebuilt and renamed the X-1E). The X-1B was fitted with special instrumentation for exploratory aerodynamic heating tests. It had over 300 thermo-couples installed on it. It was also the first aircraft to fly with a reaction control system, a prototype of the control system used on the X-15 and other manned aircraft.

The X-1D was destroyed in an explosion on a captive flight aboard a B-50 mother-ship in August 1951. 'Pete' Everest, the pilot, managed to scramble back into the B-50 before the burning X-1D was jettisoned. The explosion proved fortuitous because only half the liquid oxygen supply had been loaded and this would have caused an imbalance in flight leading to an uncontrollable spin. The loss of the X-1D and the resulting investigation delayed the introduction of the X-1A and X-1B by almost two years.

*The single Douglas X-3 Stiletto, at Muroc. Failure of the J46 engine development programme was responsible for the X-3's inability to reach its Mach 2 design objective. (McDonnell Douglas)*

# THE QUEST FOR SPEED

**Right** *Miles Hawk Speed 6, one of three built in the mid-1930s, lands at Old Warden. (Author)*

**Right** *Ray Hanna's Curtiss P-40 Kittyhawk roars to a high speed finish during the 1986 Cranfield Formula One Race. (Author)*

**Below** *In 1947 F4U Corsairs broke the closed course record during the Cleveland Air Races and they are still raced today. These CAF Corsairs were pictured at the annual Confederate Show at Harlingen, Texas in October 1986. (Author)*

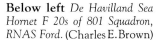

**Left** *The de Havilland Comet Racer. Note the tail wheel in place of the skid. Following a ground loop at Hatfield on 4 July 1987 a tail lock has been fitted.* (Author)

**Below left** *De Havilland Sea Hornet F 20s of 801 Squadron, RNAS Ford.* (Charles E. Brown)

**Above right** *Air Ceylon de Havilland Comet 4 airliner pictured at Singapore in the early 1960s.* (Jerry Cullum)

**Right** *Canberra B2-Ts at RAF Marham, Norfolk, on 23 September 1981.* (Author)

**Left** The BAC 221 research aircraft was modified from the airframe of Fairey Delta FD2 (WG774) to flight test the delta-wing planform designed for Concorde and is now on display at RNAS Yeovilton. (Author)

**Right** The general Dynamics F-106 Delta Dart. (USAF)

**Right** Grumman F8F Bearcat at the Confederate Air Show in October 1986. On 16 August 1969 Darryl Greenamyer in his much modified Bearcat, 'Conquest II', broke the thirty year old piston engine world air speed record with a speed of 483.041 mph (777.8 km/h). (Author)

**Below** Hawker Sea Fury FB 11 of the RNAS Yeovilton's Historic Aircraft Flight which had to be ditched off Scotland in 1989 after an undercarriage leg failed to lower. (Author)

**Left** *Two Hunter FGA 9s of No 45 Squadron.* (BAe)

**Below** *Canadian-built CF-104 Starfighter firing off a salvo of rockets.* (Canadair)

**Right** *SR-71A turning on the power.* (Author)

**Below** *Four of the F15E version of the Eagle.*

**Left** *McDonnell Douglas FA-18C Hornets from Fighter Attack Squadron (VFA-86). (McDonnell Douglas)*

**Left** *F-100F Super Sabre of the Royal Danish Air Force lifts off from RAF Coltishall during an exchange visit. (Author)*

**Left** *Tornado GR Mk 1 of No 617 'Dambusters' Squadron at RAF Marham in June 1986. (Author)*

Meanwhile, other X-aircraft were under test at Edwards. The XF-92A, which was first flown by Chuck Yeager on 18 September 1948, was the first American delta-wing aircraft and was used to obtain data on the flight characteristics of a delta-wing aircraft in the transonic speed range. The XF-92A was originally designed to take a ram-jet but was powered by an Allison J-33-A afterburning jet engine of 7,500 lb (3,409 kg) thrust. Stability and control, pitch-up and lift-drag measurements obtained from the XF-92A helped build up the technology that was used to develop such delta-wing aircraft as

the F-102, F-106 and the B-58. In October 1953 the XF-92A, with NACA pilot Scott Crossfield at the controls, collapsed on the lake bed near Edwards while taxi-ing after landing and ground looped. It was never flown again.

The X-4, low swept-wing, semi-tail-less aircraft was designed and built by Northrop to obtain in-flight data on the stability and control of semi-tail-less aircraft at high subsonic speeds. Two X-4 aircraft were built, powered by two Westinghouse XJ-30 turbojet engines, each with 1,600 lb (727 kg) thrust. These engines boosted the X-4 up to speeds of 620 mph (998 km/h) and altitudes of 40,000 feet 12,195 m).

The X-4 had made its first flight on 16

**Below** *Bell X-2 in position beneath the B-50 mother ship. The X-2 attained Mach 2.93 in July 1956. (Bell)*

December 1948 with Charles Tucker, a Northrop test pilot, at the controls. The X-4 helped demonstrate that tail surfaces are important for proper control effectiveness in the transonic speed range and was also used to investigate the characteristic problems of tail-less aircraft at low speeds, such as marginal longitudinal stability and control.

The single Douglas X-3 Stiletto, which had made its first flight in October 1952, was built to investigate the design features of an aircraft suitable for sustained supersonic speeds. A secondary purpose of the aircraft was to test new materials such as titanium. The X-3 was powered by two Westinghouse XJ-35 afterburning turbojets and was capable of take-off and landing under its own power. It possessed a top speed of just over Mach 1 and reached an altitude of 41,318 feet (12,596 m).

The X-1A was the first to resume supersonic research after the destruction of the X-1D. On 12 December 1953 Chuck Yeager flew the X-1A up to a speed of 1,612 mph (2595 km/h) (almost two and a half times the speed of sound). On 4 June Yeager reached a speed of Mach 2.42. Then on 26 August 1954 Major Ar-

thur 'Kit' Murray took the X-1A up to an altitude of 90,440 feet (27,573 m). In August 1955 the X-1A was also destroyed after being jettisoned from the carrier aircraft because of an explosion. The X-1B was flown for the first time, by Major 'Kit' Murray, in October 1954.

Meanwhile, Bell had been developing the X-2 swept wing aircraft which was designed to fly three times faster than the speed of sound. Its mission was to investigate the problems of aerodynamic heating and stability and control effectiveness at high speeds and altitudes. Two X-2s were built. They were constructed primarily of stainless steel to withstand the enormous frictional heat and each windshield was tinted to resist solar radiation. A skid-type main landing gear was installed to make room for more fuel and an ejectable nose capsule was fitted.

As aircraft like the X-2 grew in complexity, funding by the USAF lagged behind development. The two main areas of complexity were the highly sophisticated control system (hastily replaced with cable controls) and the 15,000 lb (6,818 kg) thrust Curtiss-Wright XLR25-CW-3 two-chambered rocket engine. When the first

**Right** *Bell X-5, the first swing-wing aircraft to fly, on 20 June 1951.* (Bell)

**Below left** *Swept-wing Bell X-2 stowed beneath the B-50 for an air-launched flight. On its fatal last flight in September 1956 the pilot, Mel Apt, was killed.* (Bell)

X-2 finally arrived at Edwards AFB in June 1952 below the belly of a B-50 mother-ship it was minus the engine. The X-2 was dogged with misfortune. That same month the X-2-I, with Bell test pilot Jean L. 'Skip' Ziegler at the controls, was released into a glide from the B-50 with concrete ballast in place of the rocket motor. Its nose wheel failed on touchdown at Rogers Dry Lake.

Jean Ziegler had piloted the X-5 on its first flight on 20 June 1951. The X-5 was the first aircraft capable of sweeping its wings in flight. The wings could be swept back 20° to 60°. Its mission was to study the effect of wing-sweep angles of 20°, 45° and 60° at subsonic and transonic speeds. Results from these tests pro-

vided some of the design background for the F-111 and the F-14 Tomcat.

Two X-5s were built by Bell and each was powered by an Allison J-45-A jet engine with a static thrust of 4,900 lb (2,227 kg). Each aircraft weighed 10,000 lb (4,545 kg) when fully fuelled and ejection seats were fitted as standard. Results of this research programme provided a significant full-scale verification of NASA wind-tunnel predictions for the reduced drag and improved performance resulting from increasing the wing sweep as the speed of the aircraft approached the speed of sound. The pilots found they could use the variable wing sweep as a tactical control to out-perform accompanying escort aircraft during research missions.

*The Bell X-1 was rebuilt and renamed the X-1E and is now on permanent display at the NASA facility at Edwards AFB, California.* (Author)

# FAIREY FD DELTA 1/2

**Type**: *Research aircraft* **Crew**: *Pilot only* **Manufacturers**: *Fairey Aviation Co Ltd* **Power Plant**: *One 10,050 lb st (4,568 kg) Rolls-Royce Avon RA 28 turbojet* **Dimensions**: *Span, 26 ft 10 in (7.95 m); Length, 51 ft 7½ in (15.77 m); Height, 11 ft (3.35 m)* **Weight**: *Loaded, 13,400 lb (6,090 kg)* **Performance**: *See text*

Ziegler was killed in May 1953 during captive fuel tests aboard a B-50 over Lake Ontario in the X-2-II. The experimental aircraft was jettisoned into the lake. On its first glide flight in August 1954 the second X-2-I, in the hands of 'Pete' Everest, ground looped at high speed after there were problems once again with the nose wheel. Everest made the first powered flight in the X-2 in November 1955. In July 1956 Captain Iven Kincheloe USAF reached Mach 2.93 and on 7 September he took the X-2 to an altitude of 126,200 feet (38,475 m). On 27 September the X-2 programme ended when Captain 'Mel' Milburn Apt USAF piloted the X-2 to its highest speed of 2,094 mph (3,370 km/h) (over three times the speed of sound for the first time) before it went out of control and crashed, killing the pilot.

The experimental vehicles X-6 to X-14 were mostly unmanned missiles.

The Miles M 52, which was officially commissioned in 1943, is acknowledged as Britain's first supersonic aircraft but the entire project was cancelled by the British Government in February 1946, just as the first of three prototypes was half completed. The projected design speed of 1,000 mph (1,609 km/h) at 36,000 feet (11,000 m) — after a dive from 50,000 feet (15,240 m) — was later vindicated by test models built and flown by Vickers in 1947-48.

With Britain lagging far behind in supersonic design the Fairey company set about building a delta winged aircraft under a Ministry of Supply contract to investigate the charac-

**Above** *The stubby Fairey Delta FD 1 VX350 in flight.* (Fairey Aviation)

**Right** *Fairey Delta FD 2 with droop snoot nose lowered for landing during the 1958 Farnborough Air Show.* (John Hosford)

teristics of flight and control at transonic and supersonic speeds in level flight. The design was a single-seat, mid-wing delta that was to be powered by a Rolls-Royce Avon RA 14R incorporating an afterburner with an eyelid nozzle. The first model to appear was the stubby Fairey FD 1 with a wing span of only 19 feet 6½ inches.

Two FD 2 versions followed, which differed in many respects from the earlier FD 1. The FD 2 had a wing of exceptionally thin section, and a 'droop snoot' nose was devised whereby the whole nose and cockpit could be hinged downwards by 10° to overcome restricted forward vision from the cockpit during take-off, taxi-ing and landing. This innovation was later used on Concorde and the Tu-144 supersonic airliners.

Test pilot Peter Twiss piloted FD 2 (WG774)

on its first flight on 6 October 1954. In August 1955 it achieved supersonic status. That same month the USA captured the world air speed record in the F-100C Super Sabre. Twiss piloted the second FD 2 (WG777) on its maiden flight on 15 February 1956 and took it through the sound barrier at its first attempt. Britain decided it would make an attempt on the world air speed record. At Chichester, Sussex on 10 March 1956 Peter Twiss in WG774 broke the record with a mean speed of 1,132 mph (1821.39 km/h) at 38,000 feet (11,585 m), exceeding the previous record by more than 300 mph (483 km/h).

*Fairey Delta FD 2 landing at Farnborough on 1 September 1958* (John Hasford).

Fairey Delta FD 2 (WG777) alone made 429 flights in all before the entire project was shelved in 1957. The BAC 221 research aircraft was modified from the airframe of WG774 to flight test the delta-wing planform designed for the Concorde. The nose was extended by six feet and the wing area was increased from 360 square feet to approximately 500 square feet. It flew for the first time on 1 May 1964 and was powered by a 10,050 lb st (4,568 kg) Rolls-Royce Avon RA 28R afterburning turbojet.

# FLYING BOATS

**Types**: *Flying-boats and amphibious aircraft* **Manufacturers**: *(Beriev M10 and Be-12) Design Bureau of Georgi Mikhailovich Beriev, Taganrog, Soviet Union. (Saunders-Roe SR A/1) Saunders-Roe, East Cowes, Isle of Wight, England. (Martin P6M Seamaster) Martin Marietta Aircraft Co, USA. (Shin-Meiwa PS-1) Shin-Meiwa Industry Co, Japan* **Power plants and Performance**: *see text*

Seaplanes first demonstrated their speed capabilities during the Schneider Trophy contests between 1914 and 1931. Then in October 1934 the Italian Macchi-Castoldi MC 72 set a world speed record of 440.69 mph (709.07 km/h) which would not be broken by another seaplane for almost thirty years.

Many fast seaplanes and amphibious aircraft were built during this time but it was not until the 1950s that true high-speed machines emerged. The British Saunders-Roe company

*The Saunders Roe SR A/1, the world's first jet fighter flying boat.* (Charles E. Brown)

had built three massive ten-engined prototype Princess flying-boats during 1943-53 before development of landplane commercial airliners brought the project to an end.

The same company designed and built the SR A/1, which was the world's first jet fighter flying boat. Originally, the SR A/1 had been planned for service in the Pacific in World War Two. Powered by two Metrovick Beryl turbojets, the SR A/1 had a top speed of more than 500 mph (805 km/h). However, development was protracted and by the time the first of the three test aircraft flew in 1947 its speed advantage had been eroded by land based fighters.

Two Martin XP6M-1 four-jet patrol flying boats were built as prototypes of a bomber and mine-layer for the US Navy in 1952. The engines were mounted in pairs in nacelles on the upper surface of the wing. With a span of 100 ft (30.48 m) this all-metal craft had a swept monoplane wing, a pressurized flight deck and ejection seats for all four crew. Its combat radius of 1,500 miles (2,415 km) could be extended by flight refuelling.

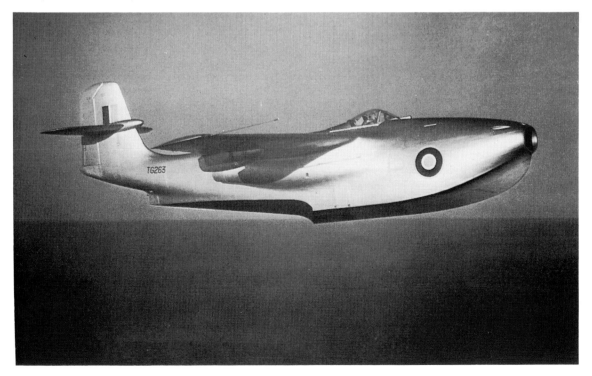

The first of two prototype XP6M-1s flew on 14 July 1955 but both were destroyed in fatal crashes. Development continued with six YP6M-1 prototypes and although 24 P6M-2s were ordered only four production P6M Seamasters had been built when the programme was abandoned in August 1959 in favour of carrier-based aircraft. However, the Seamaster briefly became the fastest flying-boat ever built with a top speed of 646 mph (1040 km/h).

Several of the world's air forces, such as Japan and the Soviet Union, continue to operate flying boats. The Japanese Maritime Self-Defence Force operates the Shin Meiwa PS-1 four-turboprop anti-submarine and search-and-rescue flying boat and amphibian. The PS-1 is powered by four licence-built 2,850 hp General Electric T64 turboprops which give a high maximum speed of 340 mph (547 km/h). The aircraft employs a boundary layer control system and it has a long, narrow, aerodynamic hull which also enables it to operate in very rough water.

The official flying boat speed record is held by a Soviet Beriev M-10 (known by its NATO codename 'Mallow'), set by Nikolay Andreyevskiy and a crew of two on 7 August 1961 with a speed of 566.69 mph (912 km/h) over a 15–25 km course. The all metal Be 10 had a swept wing of 50° at the leading edge and was powered by two 14,330 lb (6,500 kg) thrust Lyulka AL-7PB turbojets contained in large nacelles beneath the wing roots. Although the type never saw major operational service it holds all twelve records listed for jet-powered flying boats, including an altitude of 49,687 feet (14,962 m) set by Georgiy Buryanov and crew over the Sea of Azov on 9 September 1961.

During 1964, 1968 and 1972–73 the Beriev Be-12 Tchaika (Seagull) amphibian set a number of world records, including an altitude record in its class of 39,976 feet (12,185 m). Span is about 108 feet (32.90 m) and power is provided by two 4,000 shp Ivchenko A1-20D turbo-prop engines which give a top speed of around 379 mph (610 km/h). The B-12 first flew in 1960 and is still in service with units of the Soviet forces in the maritime reconnaissance role. Its NATO codename is 'Mail'.

**Left** *Beriev Be-12 Tchaika (Seagull) amphibian, of the type which set a number of world records including an altitude record in its class. (US Navy)*

**Above** *Beriev Be-12 Tchaika amphibian which is known by its NATO codename 'Mail'. (US Navy)*

**Below** *Beriev M-10, of the type which Nikolay Andreyevskiy and a crew of two set a new seaplane record on 7 August 1961 over a 15–25 km course. (US Navy)*

*Shin Meiwa PS-1s of the Japanese Maritime Self-Defence Force. (Shin Meiwa)*

# GENERAL DYNAMICS F-102A DELTA DAGGER

**Type**: *Supersonic interceptor* **Crew**: *Pilot only* **Manufacturers**: *Convair Aerospace Division of General Dynamics Corporation, San Diego, California* **Power Plant**: *One Pratt & Whitney J57-P-23A/25 turbojet, 10,000 lb (4,545 kg) thrust (17,200 lb (7,802 kg) with afterburning)* **Dimensions**: *Span, 38 ft 1½ in (11.6 m); Length, 68 ft 5 in (20.83 m); Height, 21 ft 2½ in (6.45 m)* **Weights**: *Empty, 19,050 lb (8,630 kg); Loaded, 31,500 lb (14,288 kg)* **Performance**: *Max speed, Mach 1.3 (825 mph (1,328 km/h) at 36,000 ft (10,975 m); Service ceiling, 54,000 ft (16,460 m); Range, 1,350 miles (2,172 km)* **Armament**: *Three Hughes AIM-4C/D Falcon air-to-air missile and one AIM-26A/B air-to-air missile carried internally*

The F-102 Delta Dagger was the world's first supersonic all-weather interceptor when it entered service with Air Defense Command in June 1955. Its development started in 1945, when the USAF anticipated the day when bombers would strike at supersonic speeds to launch mass destruction bombs from high in the stratosphere.

The Consolidated Vultee Corporation made exploratory design studies and the world's first delta-winged aircraft, the experimental XF-92A, resulted. It made its first flight at Muroc (now Edwards AFB), California, on 18 September 1948. Although underpowered the XF-92A proved the advantages of the delta wing over conventional straight wing or swept wing designs.

In 1950 the USAF asked manufacturers to submit designs for a faster-than-sound interceptor. The Convair Division of General Dynamics submitted a scaled-up version of the XF-92A called the YF-102. It was the most radical design and was accepted. The first YF-102 flew at Edwards AFB on 24 October

*F-102A 56-1041 Delta Dagger interceptor.* (General Dynamics)

F-102A 55-3358 *Delta Dagger of the Air Defense Command.* (General Dynamics)

1953 and the second prototype made its first flight on 11 January 1954. The YF-102 failed to reach the specified supersonic speed and led to sweeping changes in design and power. The J57-P-11 was replaced with the J57-P-23 turbojet, the YF-102's fuselage was pinched in to conform to the area rule principle and the nose was lengthened. Tail section fillets and shock engine air inlets were added and the cockpit canopy was narrowed.

The first of four YF-102As flew on 20 December 1954 and achieved supersonic flight on its second flight. The Hughes sophisticated MG-3 fire control system and the Falcon

missile were fitted to the F-102. In 1957 Convair modernized all early F-102As. Provision was made for drop tanks and a larger tail was fitted while the J57-P-23 replaced the earlier turbojet and the MG-3 fire-control system was replaced with the MG-10.

In all, 975 F-102As were built and served first-line units of Air Defense Command until 1974, when surviving aircraft were assigned to Air National Guard units.

# GENERAL DYNAMICS F-106A/B DELTA DART

**Type**: *Supersonic interceptor* **Crew**: *Pilot only* **Manufacturers**: *Convair Aerospace Division of General Dynamics Corporation* **Power Plant**: *One Pratt & Whitney J75-P-17 turbojet, 24,500 lb thrust with afterburning (11,130 kg)* **Dimensions**: *Span 38 ft 3½ in (11.67 m); Length, 70 ft 8¾ in (21.55 m); Height, 20 ft 3¼ in (6.15 m)* **Weights**: *Empty, 23,646 lb (10,725 kg); Loaded, 38,250 lb (17,350 kg)* **Performance**: *Max speed, Mach 2.3 (1,525 mph (2,455 km/h)) at 40,000 ft (12,195 m); Service ceiling, 57,000 ft (17,375 m). Range, 1,700 miles (2,735 km)* **Armament**: *One AIR-2A/B Genie unguided nuclear-warhead rocket and four AIM-4F/G Falcon air-to-air missiles carried internally; 20 mm gun*

*F-106 Delta Dart lifting off. (General Dynamics)*

The F-106 was a heavily modified F-102 Delta Dagger and was to have been the F-102B but the changes became so extensive that it was eventually re-designated the F-106. Although the two aircraft look similar and the delta wing was retained, the fuselage shape of the F-106 was highly modified to accomodate the Pratt & Whitney J75 turbojet in place of the F-102's J57 engine. This placed the aircraft's engine intakes behind the cockpit and nearer the engine. The fin and rudder were squared off and a new undercarriage was fitted.

The F-106A was flown for the first time from Edwards AFB by R.L. Johnson on 26 December 1956. Deliveries to Air Defense Command were begun in July 1959, replacement of the F-102 continuing until 1960.

On 16 December 1959 an F-106A set a new official world speed record of 1,525.95 mph (2,455.74 km/h) over a straightway course of 15 to 25 kilometres at Edwards AFB, California. Major Joseph W. Rogers of Air Defense

F-106 Delta Dart of Air Defence Command in flight.
(General Dynamics)

Command bettered by 122 mph (196 km/h)
the previous official world record of 1,404.09
mph (2,259.18 km/h) set on 16 May 1958 by an
F-104A. He also exceeded the speed record of
1,483.83 mph (2,387.48 km/h) claimed on 31
October 1959 by the Soviet Union for its new
Sukhoi Type E-66 delta-wing fighter.

# GLOSTER
# METEOR I-IV

**Type**: *Fighter* **Crew**: *Pilot only* **Manufacturers**:
*Gloster Aircraft Company; Some F 4s Subcontracted by
Armstrong Whitworth* **Power Plant**: *(F 1) Two Rolls-
Royce Welland centrifugal turbojets; (F 4) Two Rolls-
Royce Derwent 5* **Dimensions**: *(F1) Span, 43 ft (13.1
m); Length, 41 ft 4 ins (12.6 m); Height, 13 ft (3.96 m)*
**Weights**: *(F1) Empty, 8,140 lb (3,693 kg); Loaded,
13,800 lb (6,260 kg)* **Performance**: *Max speed, (Mk I)*

*410 mph (660 km/h) at 30,000 ft (9,146 m); Service ceiling, 40,000 ft (12,192 m); (F 4) 550 mph (885 km/h) at 30,000 ft (9,146 m); Service ceiling, 50,000 ft (15,243 m)*
**Armament**: *(F 1 and F 4) Four 20 mm Hispano cannon*

Towards the end of the Second World War German jet fighters such as the Me 262 and rocket fighters like the Me 263 were seen regularly by Allied bomber crews. Britain was not far behind in jet fighter design and by 1945 had gained a world lead which was not seriously challenged by America until 1947.

The Gloster G 41 was designed to specification F 9/40, drawn up in August 1940 after consultation with George Carter of Glosters by the Air Ministry. It was finally issued in December 1940, just five months before the maiden flight of the Gloster G 40 (E 28/39) experimental single-jet prototype whose power plant was designed by Frank (later Sir Frank) Whittle. Carter decided upon a twin-engined layout because of the relatively low thrust available in the early type of turbojet engine. On 7 February 1941 twelve F 9/40 prototypes were ordered from Glosters and it was intended that various types of engines would be used in these prototypes. Several British companies were engaged in jet engine research, including the pioneer firm of Power Jets Ltd. Rover and Metrovick were building the prototype power plants.

The first Meteor to be completed was fitted with Rover-built W 2B turbojets but the engines failed to produce more than 1,000 lb (454 kg) of thrust each and made only taxi-ing trials. At the control was P.E.G. Sayer, who on 15 May 1941 had made the first flight by a British powered jet propelled aircraft when he piloted the E 28/39 at Cranwell. It was not until 5 March 1943 that the fifth prototype, powered by Halford H I turbojets (forerunner of the de Havilland Goblin), each of which developed 1,500 lb (681 kg) thrust, became the first Meteor to achieve sustained flight. Work on the remaining prototypes continued throughout 1943, their number having been reduced to eight. The powerplant finally chosen was the Rolls-Royce W 2B/23 Welland of 1,700 lb (772 kg) thrust. The fourth prototype using these engines was first flown on June 12 1943 at Barford St John.

By the end of 1943 five prototype Meteors had flown, two of which had been powered by the Welland. The first production Meteor Mk I was sent to the USA in February 1944 in exchange for a Bell YP-59 Airacomet as part of an Anglo-American agreement reached in mid-1943. An order was placed by the Air Ministry for twenty Meteor Mk Is and the type

began equipping No 616 Squadron at Culmhead on July 12 1944 for future operations against V1 flying bombs.

The first 15 Meteor IIIs were fitted with Welland engines but subsequent batches were fitted with the new 2,000 lb (909 kg) thrust Derwent 1, which became standard equipment on all later Meteors.

In 1945 the RAF High-Speed Flight was reformed and equipped with two Gloster Mèteor IVs for an attempt on the air speed record set before the war. At Moreton Valence on 19 October Squadron Leader P. Stanbury DFC raised the record to 603 mph (970.23 km/h). On 7 November at Herne Bay, Kent, Group Captain H.J. Wilson AFC established a new world air speed record of 611.20 mph (983.42 km/h) flying a Meteor IV. The Meteor F IV differed from the Mk III in having uprated Derwent 5 engines.

*F 4 Meteors of No 222 Squadron, RAF Leuchars, crossing the Firth of Forth.* (Jerry Cullum)

In 1946 three additional Meteor IVs were supplied to the High-Speed Flight for a further attempt on the record. These differed from the earlier Meteors in having their wings clipped from 43 feet to 37 feet, 2 inches. This modification, which was later incorporated in almost all Meteor IVs, gave greater performance and also improved the rate of roll. On 7 September 1946 at Rustington, Sussex, Group Captain E.M. Donaldson DSO, AFC increased the record to 623.45 mph (1,003.31 km/h) in a Meteor IV.

On 4 April 1950 Janusz Zurakowski established a new Copenhagen to London record of 1 hour, 11 minutes, 17 seconds with an average speed of 501.42 mph (805.75 km/h) in a Gloster Meteor.

# GRUMMAN CATS

Since the early thirties the name Grumman has been synonymous with US Navy fighters. In 1938 the company capitalized on its long standing experience of fighters for the US Navy by moving into the multi-engine fighters for carrier deck operation. The XF5F-1 (Grumman G-45) provided a useful basis for development when in June 1941 the Navy ordered a larger twin-engined fighter. The first of two XF7F-1s flew in December 1943 and deliveries of the Tigercat commenced in April 1944. Operational problems dogged the Tigercat's early service life and only 34 single seat versions were delivered to the USMC before production switched to two-seat night-fighter versions. Although it never saw action in the Second World War the F7F served with a few Marine squadrons after the war and production continued until late 1946.

Grumman had better fortune with their Wildcat and Hellcat Navy fighters and their claim to fame initially began in the Pacific. The F6F Hellcat carrier-borne day/night fighter was designed as a replacement for the Grumman Wildcat in the US Navy service and first took to the air at Bethpage, Long Island, on 26 June 1942. The F6F first entered combat with VF-5 US Navy Squadron of USS *Yorktown* and VF-9 of USS *Essex* on 31 August 1943 with strikes against Marcus Island. Thenceforth the Hellcat showed a marked superiority against Japanese aircraft, serving with the majority of US Navy and Marine Corps squadrons in the Pacific Theatre.

By the close of 1943 approximately 2,500 Hellcats had been delivered to operational squadrons. Almost 75 per cent of all the US Navy's air-to-air victories were attributed to the F6F, with a ratio of 19:1, destroying 4,947 enemy aircraft plus another 209 claimed by land-based units. The pinnacle of its glittering Pacific career was reached during the Battle of

## GRUMMAN CAT SERIES SPECIFICATION

| Model | Span | Length | Height | Weights (Empty) (Loaded) | Powerplant | Performance | | | Armament |
|---|---|---|---|---|---|---|---|---|---|
| | | | | | | Max Speed | Service Ceiling | Range (miles) | |
| 7F Tigercat | 51 ft 6 in | 45 ft 4 in | 16 ft 7 in | 16,270 lb 25,720 lb | Two 2,100 hp R-2800-34W | 435 mph at 22,000 ft | 40,700 ft | 1,200 | Four 20 mm guns and four .5 in guns, up to 1000 lb under each wing; one torpedo under fuselage |
| 6F Hellcat | 42 ft 10 in | 33 ft 7 in | 13 ft 1 in | 9,238 lb 15,413 lb | One 2,000 hp R-2800-10W | 380 mph at 23,400 | 37,300 ft | 945 | Six .5 in guns (or two 20 mm and four .5 inch guns) |
| 8F Bearcat | 35 ft 10 in | 28 ft 3 in | 13 ft 10 in | 7,070 lb 12,947 lb | One 2,100 hp R-2800-34W | 421 mph at 19,700 | 38,700 ft | 1,105 | Four .5 in guns (F8F-1B) four 20 mm cannon |
| 9F Panther | 38 ft 0 in | 38 ft 10 in | 12 ft 3 in | 10,147 lb 18,721 lb | One 6,250 lb J48-P-6A | 579 mph at 5,000 | 42,800 ft | 1,300 | Four 20 mm cannon |
| 9F Cougar | 34 ft 6 in | 44 ft 5 in | 12 ft 3 in | 20,600 lb | One 7,200 lb J48-P-8A | 705 mph at sea level | 50,000 ft | 600 | Two 20 mm cannon |
| 11 Tiger | 31 ft 7½ in | 46 ft 2½ in | 13 ft 2¼ in | 13,428 lb 22,160 lb | One 7,450 lb J65-W-18 | 750 mph at sea level | 41,900 ft | 1,270 | Four 20 mm cannon, Four Sidewinder 1A or 1C air-to-air missiles |
| 14 Tomcat | 68° sweep 38 ft 2 in 20° sweep 64 ft 1½ in | 61 ft 2 in | 16 ft 0 in | 37,500 lb 72,000 lb | Two 20,900 lb TF30 412A | 1,564 mph (Mach 2.34). 910 mph at sea level | 56,000 ft + | 2,000 | One 20 mm M61-A1 multi-barrel cannon, four AIM-7 Sparrow or eight AIM-9 Side – winder air-to-air missiles, up to six AIM-54 Phoenix and two AIM-9 Sidewinders |

## GRUMMAN CAT SERIES SPECIFICATION (METRIC)

| Model | Span | Length | Height | Weights (Empty) (Loaded) | Powerplant | Performance | | | Armament |
|-------|------|--------|--------|--------------------------|------------|-------------|---|---|----------|
| | | | | | | Max Speed | Service Ceiling | Range (km) | |
| F7F Tigercat | 15.73 m | 13.84 m | 5.09 m | 7,395 kg 11,690 kg | Two 2,100 hp R-2800-34W | 700 km/h at 6,707 m | 12,408 m | 1,932 | Four 20 mm guns and four .5 in guns, up to 1000 lb under each wing; one torpedo under fuselage |
| F6F Hellcat | 12.83 m | 10.27 m | 3.99 m | 4,199 kg 7,005 kg | One 2,000 hp R-2800-10W | 611 km/h at 3,768 m | 11,371 m | 1,521 | Six .5 in guns (or two × 20 mm and four .5 in guns) |
| F8F Bearcat | 10.70 m | 8.62 m | 3.99 m | 3,213 kg 5,885 kg | One 2,100 hp R-2800-34W | 677 km/h at 6,006 m | 11,798 m | 1,779 | 4 × .5 in guns (F8F-1B) four 20 mm cannon |
| F9F Panther | 11.58 m | 11.61 m | 3.75 m | 4,612 kg 8,509 kg | One 2,840 kg J48-P-6A | 932 km/h at 1,524 m | 13,048 m | 2,093 | Four 20 mm cannon |
| F9F Cougar | 10.54 m | 13.56 m | 3.75 m | 9,363 kg | One 3,272 kg J48-P-8A | 1,135 km/h at sea level | 15,250 m | 966 | Two 20 mm cannon |
| F-11 Tiger | 9.67 m | 14.10 m | 4.03 m | 6,103 kg 10,070 kg | One 3,386 kg J65-W-18 | 1,207 km/h at sea level | 12,779 m | 2,045 | Four 20 mm cannon, Four Sidewinder 1A or 1C air-to-air missiles |
| F-14 Tomcat | 68° sweep 11.64 m 20° sweep 19.55 m | 18.65 m | 4.87 m | 17,045 kg 32,727 kg | Two 20,900 kg TF30 412A | 2,518 km/h (Mach 2.34). 1,465 km/h at sea level | 17,073 m + | 3,220 | One 20 mm M61-A1 multi-barrel cannon, four AIM-7 Sparrow or 8 AIM-9 Sidewinder air-to-air missiles, up to six AIM-54 Phoenix and two AIM-9 Sidewinders |

**Left** *Single-seater version of the Grumman F7F-3 Tigercat.* (Grumman)

**Above** *Grumman F6F Hellcat.* (Grumman)

the Philippine Sea, 19–20 June 1944, when the Hellcat effectively halted the Japanese attack on the first day, accounting for most of the 300 aircraft lost by the Japanese Air Force.

The Hellcat's 2,000 hp Pratt & Whitney Double Wasp R-2800-10W gave it a maximum speed of 371 mph (597 km/h) at 17,200 ft (5,243 m). With a range of 1,040 miles (1,674 km) at 159 mph (256 km/h) and a service ceiling of 36,700 feet (11,189 m), it was among the aircraft most feared by the Japanese in the Pacific theatre. By the time production ceased in November 1945, some 12,275 Hellcats had been produced.

Continued Grumman development resulted in the F8F-2 Bearcat in 1948, which eventually replaced the Hellcat in the line of fighters flown by the 'Blue Angels' US Navy precision flying team. Although originally designed to combat the Japanese Kamikaze attacks, the Bearcat nevertheless forged a link between the great Second World War fighters and those of the jet age. By late 1948 some 24 squadrons were equipped with the F8F-2.

The F8F had impressive performance considerably in excess of the earlier F6F Hellcat. With an initial climb rate of 4,800 feet/minute, (1,464 m/min) it could cruise at 163 mph (262 km/h) and its R-2800-34W engine gave a top speed of 421 mph (677 km/h) at 19,700 feet (6,006 m).

Although US Navy service never materialized, surplus Bearcats were used in the mid-1950s Indo-China war, having been supplied to the French Armèe de l'Air and, later, the Royal Thai Air Force. Some surviving French Bearcats served with the 514th Fighter Squadron of the Republic of Vietnam Air Force.

Including the two prototypes, a company demonstrator and Al Williams' 'Gulfhawk IV', Grumman had produced 1,265 F8Fs when pro-

**Above left** *Grumman F9F-5 Panther, the first US Navy jet fighter to be used in combat.* (Grumman)

**Left** *Grumman F9F-6 Cougar.* (Grumman)

**Above** *Grumman F9F-8 Cougar.* (Grumman)

duction ended in May 1949. It was not until late 1952 that the last F8F-2P squadron gave up its Bearcats. The Bearcat set a climb record on 20 November 1946 of 10,000 feet in 94 seconds, after a take-off run of only 115 feet. On 16 August 1969 Lockheed test pilot Darryl Greenamyer in his much modified Bearcat 'Conquest II', broke the thirty-year-old piston engine world air speed record with a speed of 483.041 mph (777 km/h).

Grumman's entry into the jet age began with the straight wing F9F-2. The first of two prototype XF-9F-2s flew on 24 November 1947. Production models were dubbed 'Panther' to perpetuate the Grumman 'Cat' family and were powered by a licence-built Rolls-Royce Nene, the Pratt & Whitney J42. Operational deliveries to the US Navy began in May 1949.

By the time the F9F-5 reached production status late in 1949, the Panther had been lengthened two feet, had acquired a taller fin, and was powered by the increased thrust J48 engine.

The first US Navy jet fighter to be used in combat, the F9F-2, went into action against North Korea on 3 July 1950, flying from the USS *Valley Forge*. An F9F-2 was also the first US Navy aircraft to down a MiG-15, this action taking place on 9 November 1950. Panthers flew more than 78,000 sorties in Korea, shooting down 15 MiGs without loss.

The F9F-6 Cougar was a swept-wing fighter version of the F9F Panther which prolonged production of the basic family for seven years. The prototype XF-9F-6 first flew on 20 September 1951. Production models showed a great leap in performance over the earlier Panther, which it replaced in many squadrons. The Cougar was also the first swept-wing aircraft to equip the 'Blue Angels' Navy aerobatic team.

Originally designated F9F-9 (as a Cougar variant) Grumman's second swept-wing jet fighter for the US Navy was subsequently redesignated F11F-1 from the sixth aircraft on. The F-11A Tiger first flew on 30 July 1954 and

*F-11A Tigers of the US Navy's 'Blue Angels' aerobatic display team which used the type for ten years.* (Grumman)

was the first aircraft to use the NACA-developed 'area rule' concept from design inception; this concept is more familiarly known as the 'Coke bottle' fuselage. It was also the first carrier-borne single-seat fighter with supersonic capability.

The Grumman attributes of simplicity and ruggedness were stressed in the design of the Tiger. The top and bottom wing skins were machine milled from single slabs of aluminium, greatly reducing the number of parts, time and expense usually involved in complex wing assembly. The wings also served as integral fuel tanks. Also installed were dual independent hydraulic power control systems, without complicated trim or mechanical back-up systems.

Deliveries to the US Navy began in March 1957. When production ended on 23 January 1959, some 201 Tigers had been built. Five first-line squadrons were equipped with the Tiger and the 'Blue Angels' aerobatic team used Tigers for more than ten years. During 1959 the Tiger began to be phased out of first-line service, being assigned to the Advanced Training Command.

Two aircraft were modified to F-11F-1F standard with the 15,000 lb (6,818 kg) thrust

J79-GE-3A engine and in 1956 one set unofficial world speed and altitude records of 1,220 mph (1,964 km/h) (Mach 1.85) at 40,000 feet (12,195 m) and reached an altitude of more than 70,000 feet.

During the early 1960s the US Navy saw a requirement for a high-performance fighter that could operate from aircraft carriers in all weathers and fly long distances, at high speed, to intercept and destroy any enemy aircraft or missile before they posed a threat to the fleet. Grumman's F-14 Tomcat was accepted by the US Navy and in February 1969 Grumman Aerospace signed the contract to build the replacement for the Navy's ageing F-4 Phantom.

After a two-year design and development period the first of twelve research and development aircraft made its maiden flight on 21 December 1970. The first production aircraft was delivered to the US Navy in June 1972 and for two years the US Navy carried out its evaluation of the type. When the Tomcat began deployment with the US Navy, with VF-1 and VF-2 initially on the aircraft carrier USS *Enterprise* in September 1974, it was the world's first operational air superiority fighter with a variable-sweep wing. Since then, some 26 F-14 squadrons have been deployed world-wide.

The F-14C introduced new avionics and weapons systems and the F-14D, which began development flight testing in the summer of 1986, has F110-GE-400 engines of 56,000 lb (25,454 kg) thrust, a vastly improved radar and advanced digital avionics. In addition, it carries new defensive ECM equipment, the JTIDS (Joint Tactical Information Distribution System) and an IRST (Infra-red Search and Track Set). Originally, 304 F-14Ds were planned but this was later reduced to 127. In addition, 38 Tomcats will be upgraded to F-14A Plus standard by installing the F110 turbofan, and a second stage, combining the engine upgrade with new radar and avionics, will bring these aircraft up to F-14D standard. The intention is to have an all F-14D force by 1998, and a total of 699 Tomcats will be reached.

# HAWKER TEMPEST

**Type**: *Fighter-bomber* **Crew**: *Pilot only* **Manufacturers**: *Hawker Aircraft Ltd. Mk II, Bristol Aeroplane Co* **Power Plant**: *(V) one Napier Sabre II. (VI) Sabre V* **Dimensions**: *Span, 41 ft (12.5 m); Length, 33 ft 8 in (10.26 m); Height, 16 ft 1 in (4.9 m)* **Weights**: *Empty, 9,100 lb (4,128 kg); Loaded, 13,500 lb (6,130 kg)* **Performance**: *Max speed, (V) 427 mph (688 km/h); (VI) 438 mph (704 km/h). Service ceiling, 37,000 ft (11,280 m)* **Armament**: *Four 20 mm Hispano cannon and eight rockets or up to 2,000 lb (907 kg) bombs*

One of the fastest piston engined aircraft of the Second World War was conceived in 1941 as the Typhoon II but so many changes were made to the basic Typhoon airframe that the new aircraft was renamed the Tempest.

It differed from the Typhoon primarily in having a new Napier Sabre EC 107C engine and a laminar-flow wing of elliptical plan form similar to the Spitfire. The thinner wing eliminated compressibility (local airflow exceeding the speed of sound) problem but changes were made later to the powerplant. In November 1941 the Air Ministry ordered two prototypes. Further changes were made, principally by adding a dorsal fillet to the fin and extending the fuselage to accommodate fuel tanks which could no longer be accommodated in the wings.

In 1942 six Tempest prototypes, with a variety of powerplants, were ordered. The Tempest I was fitted with the Sabre IV, two Mk IIs with the Bristol Centaurus IV, the Mks III and IV with a Rolls-Royce Griffon and the Mk V, which was the first to fly, on 2 September 1942, with the well-proven Sabre IIA engine. It was this variant, together with the Mk II, which first flew on 28 June 1943, which became the main production versions although the Mk I recorded a top speed of 466 mph (512 km/h) on its first flight on 24 February 1943.

The Tempest V began equipping Nos 3 and 486 Squadrons of the Newchurch Wing in April 1944 and No 56 Squadron in July 1944. Initially, these squadrons operated in Typhoon-style sweeps over Northern France

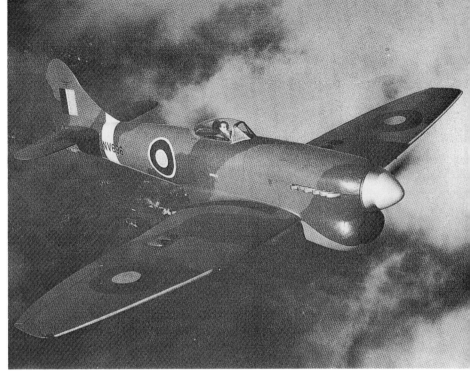

**Left** *Hawker Tempest II prototype.* (BAe)

**Right** *Hawker Tempest V with Sabre IIA engine of No 222 Squadron.* (Charles E. Brown)

**Below** *Hawker Tempest II MW742, one of 422 built by Hawker Aircraft.* (BAe)

before converting very successfully to home defence to combat the V1 threat over Southern England. Between 15 June and 5 September 1944 Tempests destroyed 638 V1s out of the RAF's total of 1,771. Tempests were also used with distinction in the final phase of the European war and by VE-Day had destroyed twenty confirmed Me 262 jet fighters in air combat.

Altogether, 800 Mk Vs were built, followed by 142 Mk VIs which introduced oil coolers in the wing and a larger radiator.

The Mk VI was intended for use in the tropics but it arrived too late to see action in the Second World War. After the war a few Mk Vs and VIs were converted to target tugs and the last was finally retired as late as 1953. The Tempest II was intended to operate with Tiger Force against the Japanese but it did not finally enter squadron service until November 1945. This was the most powerful Tempest variant, with a top speed of 440 mph (708 km/h) at 15,000 feet (4,575 m) and had a range of some 1,640 miles (2,640 km) with extra fuel tanks. Altogether, some 472 Tempest IIs were built, including 422 by Hawkers. Tempest IIs began to be replaced by the Vampire in 1949, although aircraft of No 33 Squadron served with the FEAF until 1951 when replaced by the Hornet in anti-terrorist operations in Malaya.

# HAWKER SEA FURY

**Type**: *Carrier-borne fighter bomber* **Crew**: *Pilot only* **Manufacturers**: *Hawker Aircraft Ltd, Kingston-on-Thames, Surrey* **Power Plant**: *(F B 11) One 2,480 hp Bristol Centaurus* **Dimensions**: *Span, 38 ft 4¾ in (11.7 m); Length, 34 ft 8 in (10.6 m); Height, 15 ft 10½ in (4.6 m)* **Weights**: *Empty, 9,240 lb (4,200 kg); Loaded, 12,500 lb (5,681 kg);* **Performance**: *Max speed, 460 mph (740 km/h) at 18,000 ft (5,487 m); Service ceiling, 35,800 ft (10,914 m)* **Armament**: *Four 20 mm cannon in wings and provision for twelve 60 lb rocket-projectiles or two 1,000 lb bombs below wings.*

This most powerful piston-engined fighter served with the Royal Navy from August 1947~1954 and is still in great demand today at air races throughout the world. In August 1966 a cut-down, privately owned Sea Fury flown by Mike Carroll set a new speed record for a piston-engined aircraft when he reached 520 mph (836 km/h) in level flight over Texas. It is incredible to think that the prototype Hawker Fury, which had been designed for the RAF as a Tempest replacement, first flew on 1 September 1944.

With the emergence of the Gloster Meteor interest was lost in the Fury for RAF service but a navalized version of the Fury, the F Mk X, which was developed by Boulton Paul, first flew on 21 February 1945. Deck trials carried out in May 1945 highlighted some serious handling deficiencies and led to the installation of a five-bladed Rotol propeller and other

**Below** *Hawker Sea Fury F 10 TF952.* (Hawker Siddeley)

**Right** *Hawker Sea Fury FB 11 VE790.* (Ashley Annis)

*Hawker Sea Fury FB 11 G-FURY.* (Author)

modifications for a second series of deck trials in July that year.

The first of fifty production Sea Fury F 10s flew on 30 September 1946. A total of 615 Sea Fury FB 11s were built and the last was delivered in November 1952. The aircraft's greatest claim to fame occurred during the Korean War, 1950-53, where six squadrons of Sea Furies operated from four carriers in the ground attack role. On 9 August 1952 Lieutenant P. Carmichael of No 802 Squadron flying from HMS *Ocean* claimed the Sea Fury's first MiG 15 combat kill.

At the end of the Korean War the Sea Fury gave way to the jet age and was replaced in Royal Navy service by the Sea Hawk.

# HAWKER HUNTER

**Type**: *Fighter, fighter-bomber and fighter-reconnaissance* **Crew**: *Pilot only* **Manufacturers**: *Hawker Aircraft Ltd. Produced under licence in Belgium and Holland* **Power Plant**: *One Rolls-Royce Avon turbojet* **Dimensions**: *Span, 33 ft 8 in (10.26 m); Length, 45 ft 10½ in (13.98 m); Height, 13 ft 2 in (4.26 m)* **Weights**: *Empty, 12,128 lb (5,501 kg); Loaded, 16,200 lb (7,347 kg)* **Performance**: *Max speed, 710 mph (1,144 km/h) at sea level; 620 mph (978 km/h) at altitude; Service ceiling, 50,000 ft (15,240 m); Range 490 miles (689 km), (with external tanks) 1,840 miles (2,965 km)* **Armament**: *Four 30 mm Aden cannon in gun pack below cockpit with provision for two 1,000 lb (454 kg) bombs and twenty-four 3 in rockets on underwing pylons.*

The Hunter was developed from the Hawker P 1067, which was built to Air Ministry Specification F3/48. Three prototypes were ordered

**Above** *Hawker Hunter F Mk.6 of No 92 Squadron. (BAe)*

**Right** *The record-breaking Hawker Hunter WB188. (BAe)*

**Background photograph** *Hawker Hunter FGA 9 in flight.* (BAe)

**Inset** *Ex-Royal Danish Air Force Hawker Hunter Mk 51 restored and re-registered G-HUNT, before it was sold to the Combat Jets Flying Museum in America.* (Author)

in June 1948 and the first flew on 20 July 1951 at Boscombe Down, piloted by Squadron Leader Neville Duke. Two months later the aircraft was making high speed passes in excess of 700 mph (1,127 km/h) at the Farnborough Air Show.

The second prototype flew on 5 May 1952 and introduced a gun pack containing four Aden cannon. The third flew for the first time on 30 November 1952 with a Sapphire engine in place of the 6,500 lb thrust Avon 100 and became the prototype Hunter F 2.

The first production Hunter F 1 made its maiden flight at Dunsfold, Surrey on May 16 1953. Although the early Hunters suffered engine surge problems when the guns were fired, they exhibited excellent handling qualities at all speeds and altitudes.

Some 139 F 1s were built, followed by 45 F 2s before production switched to the F 4. The F 3 designation had been applied to the original prototype Hunter in 1953 when it had been fitted with a re-heated Avon RA 7R engine. On 31 August 1953 a Hunter F 3 piloted by Squadron Leader Neville Duke unofficially set a world speed record at 741.66 mph (1,193.33 km/h) at Littlehampton, Sussex. The same pilot set a world speed record of 727.63 mph (1,170.76 km/h) on 7 September in the same aircraft.

The Hawker Hunter went on to equip the RAF both at home and abroad, taking part in the Suez Campaign in 1956 and becoming the standard mount for the 'Black Arrows' and the 'Blue Diamonds' aerobatic display teams. In 1961 the 'Blue Diamonds' assumed the mantle of the RAF's premier formation aerobatic team with its characteristic diamond nine formation.

The last Hunter FGA 9s were finally withdrawn from first-line service at the end of 1971 and the remaining FGA 9 trainers were replaced by the Hawk in 1980. The Hunter still serves with several overseas air forces including the Swiss Air Force, which currently has 126 Hunter F Mk 58s in service, having refurbished 60 aircraft in the last decade.

# LOCKHEED P-80R SHOOTING STAR

**Type**: *Fighter* **Crew**: *Pilot only* **Manufacturers**:
*Lockheed Aircraft Corporation, Burbank, California*
**Power Plant**: *(F-80C) One 4,600 lb st (2,090 kg)
J33-A-23 turbojet* **Dimensions**: *Span, 39 ft 11 ins (11.9
m); Length, 34 ft 6 ins (10.5 m); Height, 11 ft 4 ins (3.47
m)* **Weights**: *Empty, 8,240 lb (3,745 kg); Loaded,
16,856 lb (7,661 kg);* **Performance**: *Max speed, 580
mph (933 km/h) at 7,000 ft (2,134 m); Service ceiling,
42,750 ft (13,033 m)* **Armament**: *Six 5 in machine guns,
two 1,000 lb (454 kg) bombs or ten .5 in rocket projectiles*

The Lockheed P-80 Shooting Star was the first
American jet aircraft manufactured in large
quantities and the first to enter operational service with the USAF. Although it was produced
too late for World War Two, during the
Korean War of 1950-53 it was used extensively
for low level attack against ground targets.

Kelly Johnson's design team started work in
1943 around the Halford (de Havilland) H 1
Goblin turbojet, which was used in the de
Havilland Vampire fighter. Prototype construction of the design was swift and the XP-80
prototype flew for the first time on 8 January

**Above** *F-80C 49-1820 Shooting Star, one of 798 produced by Lockheed in 1948-49. The F-80 became the first USAF jet fighter to see combat when it was used in the Korean War.* (Lockheed)

**Left** *Lockheed P-80A 44-85004 Shooting Star. A specially modified P-80A captured the world air speed record on 19 June 1947.* (Lockheed)

1944. Two more prototypes, powered by the General Electric J33 engine, flew in 1944. The first YP-80A was delivered in October 1944 and two aircraft reached the Mediterranean Theatre before VE Day.

Initially, a contract was placed for 5,000 P-80s but the end of the war led to the cancellation of all but 2,000 models. A total of 917 P-80As were built, with service deliveries starting in December 1945. The F-80B, which was introduced in 1946, differed from the F-80A in having a thinner wing and a 5,200 lb st

J33-A-21 engine. That same year a P-80A (*44-85200*) was set aside for an attempt on the world air speed record, which stood at 615.78 mph (990.79 km/h) set by a British Gloster Meteor. Fitted with a water-alcohol injected J33-A-23 turbojet and with clipped wings, smaller cockpit and high-speed finish, the new aircraft was known as the XP-80B before being redesignated the XP-80R. On 19 June 1947 the XP-80R was piloted by Colonel Albert Boyd to a new world air speed record of 623.74 mph (1,003.60 km/h) at Muroc (later Edwards AFB), California. *44-85200* is now on permanent display at the Air Force Museum at Dayton, Ohio.

# LOCKHEED F-104 STARFIGHTER

**Type**: *F-104A/C, Day interceptor; F-104G, Multi-role fighter; F-104CF, strike-reconnaissance; F-104S, All-weather interceptor* **Crew** *Pilot only* **Manufacturers**: *Lockheed Aircraft Corp., Burbank, California. Also built under licence by NATO Consortium, Canadair (CF-104), Japan (F-104J) and Italy (F-104S)* **Power Plant**: *One General Electric J79 turbojet* **Specification (F-104G) Dimensions**: *Span, 21 ft 11 in (6.68 m); Length, 54 ft 9 in (16.69 m); Height, 13 ft 6 in (4.11 m)* **Weights**: *Empty, 14,082 lb (6,387 kg); Max loaded, 28,779 lb (13,054 kg)* **Performance**: *Max speed, 1,450 mph (2,330 km/h) (Mach 2.2); Service ceiling, 58,000 ft (17,680 m)* **Armament**: *(F-104S) One 20 mm M-61 Vulcan rotary cannon and two AIM-7 Sparrow III and two AIM-9 Sidewinder air-to-air missiles*

The F-104 became the first aircraft to hold the world air speed and altitude records simultaneously when in 1959 it achieved a world altitude record of 103,395 ft (31,523 m) to add to its world air speed record of 1,404.09 mph (2,259.18 km/h) set by Captain Walter W. Irvin, USAF on 16 May 1958. Also in 1958 the Starfighter had set a time-to-climb record of 266.03 seconds to reach 82,020 feet (25,006 m).

The Starfighter concept was developed following US aerial combat against Soviet-built MiG-15s during the Korean war of 1950-53 which indicated that the United States needed

**Above** F-104C Starfighters developed for service with Tactical Air Command. (Lockheed)
**Below** YF-104A 55-2969, the last of 15 built for service trials. (Lockheed)

**Right** F-104A Starfighters of Air Defence Command. On 7 May 1958 Captain Walter W. Irwin set a new world air speed record in an F-104A and the type later established seven climb-to-height records. (Lockheed)

a new jet fighter to succeed the F-80 Shooting Star and the F-86 Sabre. Among the designs considered was the Model 83 created in 1952-53 by Clarence 'Kelly' Johnson and his famed 'Skunk Works' design group at the Lockheed California Company in Burbank. The USAF accepted this proposal and the F-104 Starfighter was born. For his design work on the aircraft, Johnson received the prestigious Collier Trophy in 1959 from the American Institute of Aeronautics and Astronautics.

The first prototype rolled out of Lockheed's Burbank factory in 1953. Considered to be years ahead of its time, observers noted its extremely small wing area and downward-ejecting seat. The XF-104 flew for the first time on 7 February 1954 fitted with a General Electric J65 Sapphire with afterburner. The F-104A, which made its maiden flight ten days later, was fitted with a more powerful engine and blown flaps. On 27 April 1955 Mach 2 was achieved in a YF-104A for the first time. In its first year of service with the USAF in 1958, when it equipped Air Defense Command, the F-104A became the first operational interceptor capable of sustained speeds in excess of Mach 2.

Principally flown as fighter interceptors, three F-104s equipped with Rocketdyne AR-2 auxiliary rocket engines zoomed astronauts aloft in a training programme conducted at Edwards AFB, California, in the 1960s. On 6 June 1961 a Belgian, B.A. Neefs, set a new Brussels to Paris point-to-point speed record of 10 minutes 3.9 seconds at an average speed of 981.02 mph (1,576.43 km/h) in an F-104G.

The F-104 was still setting records in 1977 when civilian pilot Darryl Greenamyer set a new low altitude air speed record of 997 mph (1,605 km/h) in his 'home built' 'Red Baron' F-104 at Tonopah, Nevada. The aircraft was destroyed in a crash before Greenamyer could make an attempt on the high altitude record. A civilian pilot flew a Starfighter to a new world speed mark of 988.26 mph (1,591 km/h) over a three-kilometre course at restricted altitude.

Before its production run ended in 1979, the F-104 had become the most widely used Mach 2 fighter aircraft ever built. A total of 2,583 Starfighters were built by manufacturers in seven countries.

# LOCKHEED YF-12/SR-71A

*Type: YF-12, Research Interceptor; SR-71, Strategic Reconnaissance.* **Crew**: *Two* **Manufacturers**: *Lockheed-California Corporation* **Power Plant**: *Two 32,500 lb st (14,740 kg) (with afterburner) Pratt & Whitney J58 (JT11D-20B) turbojets* **Dimensions**: *Span, 55 ft 7 in (16.95 m); Length, 107 ft 5 in (32.74 m); Height, 18 ft 6 in (5.64 m)* **Weights**: *Empty, 60,000 lb (27,215 kg); Loaded, 170,000 lb (77,110 kg)* **Performance**: *Maximum speed, 2,112 mph (3,400 km/h) (Mach 3.2); Service ceiling, 86,000 ft (26,219 m); Range at Mach 3 at 78,740 ft, (24,006 m) 2,982 miles (4,801 km)*

C.L. 'Kelly' Johnson's YF-12A was a result of an advanced interceptor programme won by Lockheed in competition with Boeing, General Dynamics and North American. The winning aircraft had to be able to sustain supersonic cruise faster than Mach 3 and have a sustained altitude capability above 80,000 feet (24,400 m). An initial contract for four aircraft was awarded to Lockheed in 1960. The first three were completed as YF-12A prototypes and the fourth was modified to become the SR-71 prototype.

Built almost entirely of titanium to withstand external skin temperatures of between 450°F and 1,100°F, the aircraft is also coated with high-emissivity black paint to radiate away stored heat, which gives the aircraft its nickname of 'Blackbird'. This reduces surface temperatures by as much as 50°F. Each degree Centigrade rise in temperature results in one per cent loss in range. SR-71 crews wear space-style pressure suits of aluminium coated nylon, capable of withstanding high temperatures. The helmet has a feeding port for in-flight meals taken from bottles or tubes.

The first YF-12A made its maiden flight on 26 April 1962 at a secret location at Indian

*Colonel Robert L. Stephens and Lieutenant Colonel Daniel Andre who set a world speed record on 1 May 1965 at Edwards AFB in a YF-12A. (Lockheed)*

Springs AFB, Nevada. Three aircraft were built to interceptor standard and the fourth prototype and the first production batch of seventeen were built to SR-71 strategic reconnaissance configuration. A further order for about ten aircraft followed in 1961. The SR-71

flew for the first time on 22 December 1964 and test pilot Robert J. Gilliland took the aircraft to Mach 1.5. Deliveries to Strategic Air Command started in January 1966.

Power is provided by two Pratt & Whitney J58 turbojets, each rated at 32,500 lb (14,740 kg) thrust with afterburner at sea level. At Mach 3.2 the engine only produces 17.6 per cent of the total thrust, the inlet and ejector providing 54 and 28.4 per cent respectively. At

**Left** *Lockheed SR-71A dramatically ignites fuel during a fly-by. At least 32 Blackbirds were built (64-17950–17981) before production ceased in 1968.*

**Below** *Classic in-flight shot of the SR-71A showing to good effect the short delta wing and long chimes which contribute lift and control as well as providing space for some of the fuel and equipment.* (USAF)

maximum speed the SR-71A burns approximately 8,000 US gallons per hour. It can survey over 100,000 square miles in one hour from 80,000 feet (24,400 m) and formate on a tanker to refuel in flight at 600 mph (966 km/h).

Nine world and class records for speed and altitude were established by USAF test pilots in two YF-12 prototypes. These included a world absolute speed record of 2,070.102 mph (3,333 km/h) on 1 May 1965 set by a YF-12A from Edwards AFB piloted by Colonel Robert L. Stephens and Lieutenant Colonel Daniel Andre. Other records included an absolute sustained altitude (world and class) of 80,257.86 feet (24,478 m); 500 kilometre closed-course speed (class) of 1,643.042 mph (2,645 km/h) and a 1,000 kilometre closed-course speed (class) of 1,688.891 mph (2,719 km/h).

In April 1971 Lieutenant Colonel Thomas B. Estes and Lieutenant Colonel Dewain C. Vick flew an SR-71 on a 10½ hour non-stop, refuelled mission of about 15,000 miles to win the 1971 MacKay Trophy for 'The most meritorious flight of the year' and the 1972 Harmon International Trophy for 'The most outstanding international achievement in the art/science of aeronautics.'

On 1 September 1974 an SR-71A, *en route* to participate in the Farnborough Air Show, set a new transatlantic record of 1 hour, 54 minutes, 56.4 seconds on a 3,461 mile (5,570 km) flight from New York to London. The aircraft's average ground speed was 1,806.96 mph (2,908 km/h). On 13 September, this aircraft, with a different crew, established a world speed record of 3 hours 47 minutes and 35.8 seconds on a flight from London to Los Angeles, a distance of 5,645 miles (9,090 km). The average ground speed was 1,438 mph (2,315 km/h).

Two SR-71A crews set seven new world speed and altitude records on 27-28 July 1976 near Beale AFB, California. Captain Eldon W. Joersz and Major George T. Morgan Jr established a new world air speed record of 2,193.167 mph (3,529.56 km/h). The SR-71A also set a 1,000 kilometre closed circuit course

record of 2,092.29 mph (3,369 km/h) and an absolute/class altitude in level flight at 85,068.99 feet (2,593 m).

# MCDONNELL F-101A VOODOO

**Type:** *Interceptor fighter and tactical fighter bomber* **Crew:** *(F-101A/B) one; (F-101C) Two* **Manufacturers:** *McDonnell Aircraft Corporation (later McDonnell Douglas), St. Louis, Missouri* **Power Plant:** *Two 11,700 lb (5,318 kg) (14,500 lb (6,590 kg) with afterburning) Pratt & Whitney J57-P-13/55 turbojets* **Dimensions:** *Span, 39 ft 8 in (12.09 m); Length, 67 ft 4¾ in (20.55 m); Height, 18 ft (5.49 m)* **Weight:** *Loaded, 47,000 lb (21,363 kg)* **Performance:** *Max speed, 1,220 mph (1,963 km/h); Service ceiling, 52,000 ft (15,850 m)* **Armament:** *Three GAR Falcon air-to-air missiles in internal bomb bay and two Douglas MB-1 Genie missiles under fuselage. (F-101C) Four 20 mm cannon*

On 12 December 1957 at Edwards AFB, California, Major Adrian Drew USAF powered his F-101A Voodoo to a speed of 1,207.60 mph (1,943.03 km/h) and recaptured the world air speed record that America had surrendered to Britain's Fairey Delta in 1956. It was a quite remarkable achievement by the second of the USA's 'century fighters' which had first flown in 1948 but had been cancelled in 1950 through lack of funding.

The project was revived in 1951 when Strategic Air Command saw a need for a long-range escort fighter for the B-36 intercontinental bomber. The original XF-88, which had been designed in 1946, was improved with J57 turbojets in place of the earlier J34s and an additional fuselage bay for extra fuel.

SAC cancelled their requirement before the F-101 flew on 29 September 1954 but the aircraft continued to be developed for use by Tactical Air Command. The F-101A equipped three squadrons before the F-101C was introduced in mid-1957 with strengthened wing for low level operation and provision for an atomic weapon in place of the Falcon AAMs. The F-101B, which had first flown on 27 March 1957, was used by Air Defense Com-

mand from 1961 as a long-range interceptor. It differed from the F-101C in having a MG-13 radar fire-control operator behind the pilot in a lengthened cockpit. Altogether, some 575 Voodoos were built and about 132 ex-USAF models subsequently served with the CAF (Canadian Armed Forces).

**Left** *McDonnell F-101C of Tactical Air Command.* (McDonnell Douglas)

**Below left** *F-101C (foreground) flanked by an F-101B two-seat interceptor (left) and an RF-101C (right). On 12 December 1957 an F-101C flown by Major Adrian Drew set a new world air speed record.* (McDonnell Douglas)

**Below** *F4-K Phantom of the Royal Navy over St Louis, Missouri. On 11 May 1969 an F-4K flown by Lieutenant-Commander Brian Davies set a New York to London record of 4 hours, 36 minutes.* (McDonnell Douglas)

# MCDONNELL DOUGLAS F-4 PHANTOM II

**Type:** *All-weather fighter, ground-attack, interceptor and fighter-reconnaissance* **Crew:** *Two* **Manufacturers:** *McDonnell Douglas Aircraft Corporation, St. Louis, Missouri. (RN/RAF versions) BAC (Now BAe) Preston; rear fuselage and fin/rudder assemblies. Short Brothers, Belfast, outer wing panels* **Power Plant:** *(F-4E); Two General Electric J79-GE-17 turbojets. (RN/RAF versions); Two Rolls-Royce RB 168-25R Spey 202 turbojets* **Dimensions:** *(K,M) Span, 38 ft 5 in (11.7 m); Length, 57 ft 7 in (17.55 m); Height, 16 ft 3 in (4.96 m)* **Weights:** *(K,M) Empty, 31,000 lb (14,060 kg); Loaded, 58,000 lb (26,308 kg)* **Performance:** *Max speed (F4-E) (clean) 910 mph (1,464 km/h) (Mach 1.19) at 1,000 ft (305 m); (J79) 1,500 mph (2,414 km/h), (Spey) 1,386 mph (2,231 km/h) at 40,000 ft (12,200 m); Max range, 1,750 miles (2,817 km/h); service ceiling 60,000 ft (18,292 m)* **Armament:** *(FG I); Four Sparrow air-to-air radar guided missiles and four Sidewinder air-to-air infra-red missiles. (FGR 2): Eleven 1,000 lb free-fall or retarded bombs, 126 SNEB 68 mm armour-piercing rockets. One 20 mm Vulcan SUU 23 rotary cannon*

On 22 November 1961 the F-4 Phantom became the fastest aircraft in the USAF inventory when Lieutenant Colonel Robert B. 'Robbie' Robinson USMC attained 1,606.51 mph (2,585.43 km/h) in an F-4H at Edwards AFB, California to beat the previous record held by the F-106A. Also in 1961, Hunt Hardisty established a new low-altitude air speed record of 902.2 mph (1452 km/h) in an F-4H.

More records would follow for the Phantom, one of the US Navy's hottest jets. When the service had placed a letter of intent for a new shipboard fighter on 18 October 1954, few could have foreseen the multitude of roles this most successful of post-war fighters would fulfil. As early as 1955 changes in specification altered the Phantom's primary role from a twin-engined strike aircraft to that of a long-range, high-altitude interceptor. The XF4H-1

made its maiden flight on 27 May 1958 and delivery to the US Navy began in February 1960 for carrier trials. In all, 1,218 Phantom IIs have been supplied to the US Navy with a further 46 to the USMC.

The first Phantom to equip the USAF was the F-4C tactical fighter developed from the US Navy F-4B. The F-4C differed from the naval version in having dual controls, an inertial navigation system, J79-GE-15 turbojets and boom flight refuelling as well as provision for a large external weapons load. Altogether, 583 F-4Cs were built and served with the USAF in a variety of roles including close-support, attack and air superiority.

The F-4D was developed from the F-4C and introduced improved weapons delivery systems. The type flew for the first time in December 1965 and began equipping the

USAF in March 1966. In all, 843 F-4Ds were built and some equipped the air forces of Iran and the Republic of Korea.

The F-4E, which first flew on 30 June 1967, is a multi-role fighter designed for the close-support, interdiction and air-superiority roles. The type is fitted with a 20mm Vulcan rotary cannon and in the intercept role can carry four or six AIM-7E plus four AIM-9D air-to-air missiles. Internally, the F-4E carries an additional fuselage fuel tank, improved fire-control and target guidance systems while leading-edge slats are retro-fitted to improve manoeuvrability. The F-4G or 'Wild Weasel' is a modified F-4E with highly sophisticated electronic warfare systems for defence-suppression purposes.

Altogether, some 5,211 Phantoms have been built, including 2,712 which have been delivered to the USAF. The Phantom II serves with eight foreign air forces, including the RAF. The F4-K also served with the Royal Navy from January 1969 until 1978. On 11 May 1969 an F-4K Phantom flown by Lieutenant Commander Brian Davies set a New York to London record of 4 hours, 36 minutes with an average speed of 724.90 mph (1,165 km/h).

The RAF currently uses the FGR 2 in the air defence role in Germany and the UK while one squadron is stationed at Port Stanley for the air defence of the Falkland Islands. The Panavia Tornado F Mk 2 Air Defence Fighter has allowed some Phantoms to be retired. Those that remain in service will be effective up to the end of the decade.

*For five years the F-4J was flown by the 'Blue Angels', the US Navy Flight Demonstration Squadron. The Phantom was also flown by the Thunderbirds USAF aerobatic display team. (McDonnell Douglas)*

# MCDONNELL F-15 EAGLE

**Type**: *Air superiority fighter* **Crew**: *(F-15A/C) Pilot only; (F-15B/D) Two* **Manufacturers**: *McDonnell Aircraft Co., Division of McDonnell Douglas Corporation* **Power Plant**: *Two 23,830 lb (10,810 kg) reheat Pratt & Whitney F100-PW-100 turbofans* **Dimensions**: *Span, 42 ft 9 in (13.05 m); Length, 63 ft 9 in (19.43 m); Height, 18 ft 5½ in (5.65 m)* **Weights**: *(F-15C) Empty, 26,147 lb (11,860 kg); Loaded, 38,250 lb (17,350 kg); Max, 68,000 lb (30,909 kg)* **Performance**: *(F-15C) Max speed, 915 mph (1,473 km/h) (Mach 1.5) at sea level, 1,650 mph (2,657 km/h) (Mach 2.5) at 36,090 ft; Service ceiling, 65,000 ft (19,817 m)* **Armament**: *One 20 mm M-61A-1 rotary cannon, four AIM-9L Sidewinder and four AIM-7F Sparrow air-to-air missiles. Additional 15,000 lb external stores*

The F-15 Eagle is expected to outperform and outclass any enemy aircraft in the foreseeable future — a pre-requisite of its conception in 1967 when the prominence of the Soviet built MiG-23 and MiG-25 in the air-superiority role prompted the United States to develop a rival aircraft.

In February 1973 McDonnell Douglas received orders, on a fly-before-buy basis, for eighteen F-15As, two dual-seat TF-15A trainer development aircraft and twenty-three F-15A and seven TF-15A production models. The first F-15A made its maiden flight on 27 July 1972 and the first two-seater took to the air on 7 July 1973 (all trainers were subsequently redesignated, F-15B). The F-15A first entered service with Tactical Air Command's Training Wing at Luke AFB, Arizona, in November 1974.

In January 1975 the nineteenth F-15A pro-

**Below** *McDonnell Douglas F-15A. The F-15A flew for the first time on 27 July 1972.*

**Right** *Two F-15As of the 36th Tactical Fighter Wing based at Bitburg in formation in September 1980.* (Author)

**Below right** *Two F-15Cs based at Luke AFB, Arizona, in October 1987.* (Author)

duction model was stripped down for world record attempts. The Streak Eagle established eight world time-to-height records, including a climb to 39,372 feet (12,000 m) in just 59 seconds, which beat the previous record of 77 seconds set by an F-4. The F-15 also established a record climb to 98,439 feet (30,000 m) in 207 seconds, beating the record set previously by a MiG 25 (which recaptured this record shortly afterwards).

The F-15A first entered service with the 1st TFW at Langley AFB in January 1976. The F-15C, which made its maiden flight on 26 February 1979, differs from the F-15A in having increased fuel capacity, FAST packs on the fuselage sides and enhanced radar capability. Israel, Japan and Saudi Arabia all purchased F-15C single-seat and F-15D dual-seat models. The F-15 was first used in combat by the Israeli Air Force, on 27 June 1979, when five Syrian MiG-21s were shot down.

The interdictor/strike F-15E, which first flew on 11 December 1986, is the latest version and differs from previous models in having an all-weather ground attack capability. Some 392 F-15Es are on order, which takes total USAF orders to 1,266 Eagles.

Meanwhile, an F-15B has been converted into a STOL Manoeuvring Technology Demon-strator. Known as the F-15S/MTD, it had two-dimensional thrust vectoring/reversing engine nozzles, fly-by-wire and canard foreplanes.

# MCDONNELL DOUGLAS F-18 HORNET

**Type:** *Carrier-borne and land-based strike aircraft* **Crew:** *(F-18A/C) Pilot only. (F-18B/D) Two* **Manufacturers:** *McDonnell Douglas, St Louis (prime contractor). Northrop Corporation, St Louis, Missouri (30 per cent of airframe development and 40 per cent of airframe production)* **Power Plant:** *Two 16,000 lb (7,257 kg) thrust GE F404-GE-400 turbofans* **Dimensions:** *Span, 37 ft 6 in (11.43 m); Length, 56 ft (17.0 m)* **Weight:** *Loaded, 49,224 lb (22,328 kg)* **Performance:** *Max speed, Mach 1.8+* **Armament:** *one 20 mm M61 cannon in nose, 17,000 lb (7,711 kg) of external stores including up to six AAMs or air-to-surface missiles*

On 7 October 1974 Northrop joined with McDonnell Douglas in a collaborative project to compete for a Navy/USMC contract for a lightweight, single-seat fighter to replace the F-4 Phantom, A-4 Skyhawk and A-7 Corsair with Navy and Marine squadrons. The Navy was not interested in the single-engined F-16 adopted by the USAF and further re-

**Above** *F-18 Hornet FSD (Full Scale Development) aircraft during its first flight on 18 November 1978 armed with two AIM-9L Sidewinders on the wingtips and two AIM-7F Sparrows under the engine nacelles. (McDonnell Douglas)*

**Left** *Northrop YF-17 which was later adapted to US Navy requirements and adopted as the F/A-18A Hornet. (Northrop)*

equipment with the Grumman F-14 Tomcat had been ruled out because of high cost.

Relying on McDonnell Douglas to provide the necessary experience in Naval aircraft design and build the aircraft at St Louis, Northrop entered the YF-17 twin-engined fighter, which had been beaten in the USAF Lightweight Fighter Prototype programme by the YF-16. Although additional fuel and weapons load increased its all-up weight by 10,000 lb

and required additional wing area, the YF-17, now renamed the Hornet and fitted with GE F404-GE-400 turbojets in place of the 14,800 lb thrust YF101-GE-100 engines, was still able to meet the Navy specification. It had a combat radius of 460 miles and a top speed of Mach 1.8. Epoxy-graphite composite structure as well as conventional light alloy is used in its construction and fly-by-wire technology has since been introduced.

The new fighter was accepted on 2 May 1975 and in January 1976 a contract was issued for nine F-18A single-seat and two F-18B dual-seat development aircraft. In June 1976 the A-18 attack version was announced to replace the A-7 Corsair II and in November an F-18L designation was issued for a lighter, land-based version of the Hornet. Orders were subsequently received from Australia (75), where it is built under licence, Canada (137) and Spain (72).

The first F-18A Hornet flew on 18 November 1978 at St Louis and the first production aircraft first took to the air in April 1980. Early in

*McDonnell Douglas F/A-18 Hornet from Fighter Attack Squadron (VFA-125) over Lake Tahoe. (US Navy)*

1983 the Hornet entered service with US marine fighter/attack squadron 314. In 1985 this squadron departed on USS *Constellation* for the first major deployment at sea. The first F-18C flew on 3 September 1986, with deliveries starting in September 1987.

The F-18D, which is optimized for night-attack, flew for the first time on 6 May 1988. Both the F-18C and D differ from the F-18A and B in having AIM-120 air-to-air and infra-red Maverick missiles, airborne self-protection jammers, improved computers and Martin-Baker NACES (Navy aircrew common ejection seats).

The US Navy has a total requirement for 1,150 F-18 single-seat and F-18B tandem two-seat aircraft and from 1990 83 RF-18D reconnaissance versions will replace USMC RF-4B Phantoms.

# MESSERSCHMITT Me 163B KOMET

**Type:** *Interceptor* **Crew:** *Pilot only* **Manufacturers:** *Messerschmitt AG and dispersed factories of the Hans Klemm Flugzeugbau* **Power Plant:** *One 3,750 lb (1,700 kg) st Walter HWK 109-509A-2 bi-fuel liquid rocket motor* **Dimensions:** *Span, 30 ft 7 in (9.3 m); Length, 18 ft 8 ins (5.69 m); Height, 9 ft (2.74 m)* **Weights:** *Empty, 4,191 lb (1,905 kg); Loaded, 9.042 lb (4,110 kg);* **Performance:** *Max speed, 596 mph (960 km/h); Service ceiling, 54,000 ft (16,500 m)* **Armament:** *Two Rheinmetall Borsig Mk 108 30 mm cannon*

One of the greatest surprises encountered by American daylight bomber crews in the summer of 1944 was the sight of a rapidly climbing, tail-less, rocket-powered interceptor, the first in the world, hurtling towards them with only the remotest chance of being caught by conventional Allied fighters. Fortunately for 8th Air Force bomber crews the Komet had a range of only 22 miles and only about 360 were built. Had they arrived sooner and in greater numbers their effect on the Allied bomber effort might have been more marked.

The Me 163 was designed by Dr Alexander Lippisch, who for many years had specialized in the design of tail-less gliders. Lippisch used metal construction for the fuselage but the wings were made of wood. The leading edge of the wing featured long slats in front of the elevons. After take-off the wheels were jettisoned, and for landing a skid was used. A small propeller on the nose drove a generator which supplied electrical power for the radio and instruments.

The Komet first flew as a glider in the spring of 1941 before being moved to the German research establishment at Peenemünde where a Walter HWK R 11 rocket engine was installed. The first powered flight took place in August 1941 and during trials Heini Dittmar smashed

*Alexander Lippisch's Me 163 V 2 with rounded fuselage and cockpit area.* (Heinz J. Nowarra)

*Me 163 B-1 Komet rocket interceptor.* (Heinz J. Nowarra)

the world's speed record when he attained 571 mph. On 2 October Dittmar was towed by a Bf 110 to a height of 11,810 feet where he started the rocket motor and flew the Komet at a speed of 623.8 mph (1,004 km/h) in level flight. The Me 163B flew for the first time in August 1943.

Production versions were fitted with the Walter HWK 509A bi-fuel rocket engine which used two types of fuel, 'T-stoff' (hydrogen peroxide and water) and 'C-stoff' (hydrazine hydrate, methyl alcohol and water); one being a catalyst to the other.

Only one Komet-Geschwader, 1./JG 400, was equipped with the Me 163B, with initial deliveries taking place during May–June 1944. This unit, which comprised 1 Staffel and 2 Staffel, was concentrated on Brandis in July 1944. 1./JG 400 first used its Komets in action on 16 August, against B-17 Flying Fortresses. During its short operational career many Komets were written off in accidents caused by fuel problems and landing accidents. Komets accounted for only about nine Allied aircraft before the last combat sortie on 7 May 1945.

# NORTH AMERICAN F-86 SABRE

**Type**: *Fighter-bomber and all-weather interceptor fighter* **Crew**: *Pilot only* **Manufacturers**: *North American Aviation Inc., Inglewood, California and Columbus, Ohio. Sub-contracted by Canadair Ltd., Montreal, Canada. Societa per Azioni Fiat, Turin, Italy.* **Specification (F-86A): Power Plant**: *One 5,200 lb (2363 kg) thrust General Electric J-47 GE-13.* **Dimensions**: *Span, 37 ft 1½ in (11.31 m); Length, 37 ft 6 in (11.43 m); Height, 14 ft 8¾ in (4.47 m)* **Weights**: *Empty, 10,495 lb (4,770 kg); Loaded, 16,357 lb (7,435 kg)* **Performance**: *Max speed, 675 mph (1,086 km/h) at 2,500 feet; Service ceiling, 48,300 ft (14,730 m)* **Armament**: *Six .50 calibre machine guns in nose, two 1,000 lb bombs or 16 .5 in rocket projectiles*

The F-86 Sabre was the first transonic, swept-wing jet fighter to see service in the West and the only United Nations fighter capable of meeting the MiG-15 on equal terms during the Korean War of 1950–53.

The straight-wing XJF-1 flew for the first time on 27 November 1946 but the results of German wartime research into swept wings led to a 35° sweep angle being adopted for the XP-86.

*The F-86 Sabre was one of the most famous fighters of the fifties, seeing service against MiG fighters in Korea and establishing three world air speed records between 1952 and 1953. The model shown is an F-86H. (North American)*

This aircraft made its inaugural flight on 1 October 1947 and the following spring it exceeded Mach 1, in a shallow dive, for the first time. The P-86A flew for the first time on 18 May 1948 and the following month the type was redesignated F-86A. On 15 September 1948 an F-86A piloted by Major Richard L. Johnson, USAF established a new world air speed record of 670.98 mph (1,079.61 km/h) at Muroc (later Edwards AFB) in the Mojave Desert of southern California.

Service deliveries began in December 1948 and the first unit to be fully equipped was the 1st Fighter Group at March Air Force Base, California, in March 1949. That year a TG-190 (J57) engined YF-86D broke the world speed record of 670.98 mph (1,079.61 km/h). On 19 November 1952 an F-86D piloted by Captain J. Slade Nash, USAF set a new world air speed record of 699.94 mph (1,126.20 km/h) at Salton Sea, California. On 16 July 1953 Lieute-

nant Colonel William F. Barnes, USAF in an F-86D raised the record to 715.75 mph (1,151.64 km/h) before the Hawker Hunter 3 smashed the record in September that year.

# NORTH AMERICAN F-100C SUPER SABRE

**Type**: *Supersonic interceptor and fighter-bomber* **Crew**: *Pilot only* **Manufacturers**: *North American Aviation Inc., Inglewood, California and Columbus, Ohio* **Power Plant**: *(F-100D) One 16.950 lb st (7690 kg) (with afterburner) Pratt & Whitney J57-P-21A turbojet* **Dimensions**: *Span, 38 ft 9½ in (11.81 m); Length, 47 ft (14.32 m); Height, 16 ft 2¾ in (4.96 m)* **Weights**: *Empty, 21,000 lb (9,525 kg); Loaded, 34,832 lb (15,800 kg)* **Performance**: *Max speed, 864 mph (1,390 km/h) (Mach 1.31) at 35,000 ft (10,675 m)* **Armament**: *Four 20 mm. One Pontiac M-39E cannon in front fuselage. Under-wing pylons for six 1,000 lb bombs or two Sidewinder or Martin GAM-83A Bullpup air-to-air missiles*

On 29 October 1953, the day that George Welch, the North American test pilot, was putting the first production F-100 through its paces, Lieutenant Colonel Frank Everest,

USAF established a new world air speed record of 755.15 mph (1,215 km/h) in a YF-100A at Salton Sea, California. The 'Hun' (first of the Century-series fighters) had become the world's first operational fighter capable of supersonic performance in level flight.

These achievements were the culmination of two years' project design and development work on evolving a more powerful, 45° swept-back wing version from the old F-86 Sabre design. The two YF-100As with an XJ57-P-7 engine had flown for the first time on 25 May and 14 October respectively. The first of 203 F-100As was delivered to the Tactical Air Force in late November 1953 and the 479th Fighter Wing became operational on the type in September 1954.

**Left** *North American F-100D Super Sabre. In 1953 and 1955 F-100s established two world air speed records. (North American)*
**Below** *The first production North American F-100A Super Sabre 52-5756 which flew on 29 October 1953, on the same day that Lieutenant Colonel Frank Everest in the first YF-100A established a new world air speed record at Salton Sea, California. (North American)*

The F-100A was followed into production by the F-100C, which had a strengthened wing to carry external stores in a fighter-bomber role. The new wing was fitted to an F-100A and was flight tested on 26 July 1954. On 17 January 1955 test pilot Al White flew the first production F-100C from Los Angeles. Eventually, some 476 F-100Cs were produced before production switched to the F-100D. On 20 August 1955 Colonel Harold A. Hanes, USAF piloted an F-100C to a new world air speed record of 822.27 mph (1,323.03 km/h) at Edwards AFB, California. It was the first time the record had exceeded Mach 1 and was to stand for almost seven months, until March 1956, when the Fairey Delta recaptured the record for Britain.

Although total F-100 production only reached 2,294, the Super Sabre still saw action during the war in South-East Asia where it gave outstanding service as a low level attack and high cover aircraft. It also equipped the US Thunderbirds aerobatic display team and pioneered global deployment of tactical aircraft by means of the probe and drogue aerial refuelling system.

# NORTH AMERICAN X-15A-2

**Type**: *Supersonic experimental aircraft* **Crew**: *Pilot only* **Manufacturers**: *North American Aviation* **Power Plant**: *(X-15) One Thiokol Chemical Corporation (Reaction Motors) XLR-99-RM-2 single-chamber rocket engine developing 57,000 lbs (25,909 kg) thrust at 45,000 ft (13,719 m)* **Dimensions**: *Span, 22 ft (6.70 m); Length, 50 ft (15.24 m)* **Weights**: *Empty, 14,000 lb (6,363 kg); Loaded, 34,000 lb (15,454 kg)* **Performance**: *See text.*

The X-15 research aircraft, of which three were built during the late 1950s, was a missile-shaped vehicle with an unusual wedge-shaped vertical tail, thin stubby wings and unique side fairings that extended along the side of the fuselage. It was developed to provide in-flight information data on aerodynamics, structures, flight controls and the physiological aspects of high speed, high altitude flight. A follow-on programme used the aircraft as a test bed to carry various scientific experiments beyond the earth's atmosphere on a repeated basis.

Ablative materials were applied to the fuselage, nose and wing leading edges to enable the X-15 to withstand a temperature of 1,320°C when it re-entered the earth's atmosphere. This coating then melted away to leave the main fuselage and wing structure, which was made of Inconel, a metal capable of withstanding a temperature of 2,102°C, intact.

For flight in the dense air of the usable atmosphere the X-15 used conventional aerodynamic controls. For flight in the thin air above 200,000 feet (60,975 m) the X-15 used a ballistic control system. Eight hydrogen peroxide thrust rockets located on the nose of the aircraft provided pitch and yaw control. Four other rockets were located on the wings for roll control. The rocket engine was pilot controlled.

North American had been awarded the X-15 contract in December 1955. In October 1958 the X-15-1 was delivered to Edwards AFB,

**Below** *North American X-15 pictured with Scott Crossfield, the first man in the world to fly at twice the speed of sound.* (North American)

**Right** *North American X-15. On 3 October 1967 Major William J. Knight set a world air-launched record speed in the X-15A-2.* (North American)

USAF
U.S. AIR FORCE
U.S. AIR FORCE
LIQ. OXY VENT
APU EXHAUST
APU EXHAUST

California where it made its first captive flight in March 1959 with Scott Crossfield at the controls. On 8 June Crossfield made the first glide flight. At this time the X-15 was fitted with lower-powered engines because the XL-99 was behind schedule. On 17 September 1959 Crossfield made the first powered flight in the X-15-2, which was powered by two XLR11-RM-5 engines giving a combined thrust of about 33,000 lb (15,000 kg).

Because of the large fuel consumption, the X-15 was air launched from a B-52 bomber at 45,000 feet (13,719 m) and a speed of about 500 mph (805 km/h). Depending on the mission, the rocket engine provided thrust for the first 80-120 seconds of flight. The remainder of the normal 10-11 minute flight was powerless and ended with a 200-242 mph glide landing. Generally, one of two types of X-15 flight profiles was used: a high altitude flight plan that called for the pilot to maintain a steep rate of climb, or a speed profile that called for the pilot to push over and maintain a level altitude.

In June 1960 the X-15-3 was destroyed during an engine ground test. Crossfield fortunately escaped injury. In August 1960 Joseph A. Walker flew the X-15-1 at 2,196 mph (3536 km/h) and that same month Major Robert White set a record height of 136,500 feet (41,615 m). In November Scott Crossfield, in the X-15-2, attained Mach 3, for the first time after the XLR-99 engine had been fitted in the second prototype. This engine was nine times more powerful than that used in the X-1 and on a shallow, ballistic flight profile, the X-15 was capable of flying at 75 miles a minute, or about Mach 7.0. On 22 August 1963 Joseph A. Walker reached 354,200 feet (107,987 m) and by December the X-15s had reached a speed of Mach 6.06.

Following a landing accident with the X-15-2 in 1962, this aircraft was rebuilt as the X-15A-2. A number of modifications were made to produce greatly improved performance and it was powered by a liquid oxygen and anhydrous ammonia rocket propulsion system. The X-15A-2 made its first flight on 25 June 1964 and on 3 October 1967 it captured the air-launched record with a speed of 4,534 mph (7,297 km/h) (Mach 6.72) when piloted by Major William J. Knight, USAF. The programme was suspended after the final flight, of 24 October 1968. Altogether, the three X-15 aircraft had flown a total of 199 flights.

# NORTH AMERICAN XB-70A VALKYRIE

**Type**: *Strategic Bomber* **Crew**: *Two (originally four)* **Manufacturers**: *North American Aviation Incorporated, Inglewood, California.* **Power Plant**: *Six General Electric YJ93-3 turbojets* **Dimensions**: *Span, 105 ft (32.01 m); Length, 189 ft (57.62 m); Height, 30 ft (9.14 m)* **Weight**: *Loaded, approximately 550,000 lb (250,000 kg)* **Performance**: *Max speed, Mach 3*

The XB-70 Valkyrie was the world's largest experimental aircraft, capable of flight at speeds of three times the speed of sound at altitudes of 70,000 feet (21,341 m). It was used to collect inflight information for use in the design of future military and civilian supersonic aircraft.

It was also intended as a replacement for the Boeing B-52 and as such was developed as the first Mach 3 Strategic bomber for the USAF. However, a change of policy led to its cancellation in favour of inter-continental missiles and it was decided to limit the aircraft's mission to flight research. The major objectives of the XB-70A flight research programme were to study the aircraft's stability and handling characteristics, to evaluate its response to atmospheric turbulence and to determine the aerodynamic and propulsion system performance. In addition, there were secondary objectives to measure the noise and friction associated with air flow over the aircraft and to determine the levels and extent of the engine noise during take-off, landing and ground operations.

The XB-70 was designed to make use of a little-known phenomenon called 'compression lift' which is achieved when the shock wave

*The second North American XB-70A Valkyrie (20001) which flew for the first time on 17 July 1965 but was destroyed in a mid-air collision with a chase-plane on 6 June 1966. (North American)*

generated by the shape of an aircraft flying at supersonic speeds actually supports part of the aircraft's weight. Built largely of stainless-steel honeycomb sandwich panels and titanium, the XB-70 had a long forward fuselage with a canard or horizontal stabilizer mounted just behind the crew compartment and a thin 65.5° swept delta wing. The Valkyrie could drop its wing tips as much as 65° at supersonic speeds to improve greater lateral directional stability. Two windshields were fitted; a movable outer windshield was raised for high speed flight to reduce drag and lowered for greater visibility for take-off and landing. Internal geometry of the inlets was controllable to maintain most efficient airflow to the engines.

When a design contract was awarded to North American on 23 December 1957 it was intended that the XB-70 would use Boron fuel. This idea was scrapped in 1959. The project was dogged with arguments between the proponents of the manned bomber concept and those who argued that inter-continental missiles made aircraft such as the XB-70 obsolete. Three XB-70 prototypes were finally ordered on 4 October 1961 after much political wrangling but the third prototype was cancelled in March 1963.

Two XB-70As were completed for use as research aircraft and the first was rolled out at Palmdale, California on 11 May 1964. It weighed 237 tons. It flew for the first time on 21 September 1964 and attained a speed of Mach 3 — about 2,000 mph (3,254 km/h) — on 14 October 1965. It has climbed to 70,000 feet (21,341 m). The number two XB-70 flew for the first time on 17 July 1965 but was destroyed in a mid-air collision with a chase-plane on 6 June 1966. Programme management of the NASA-USAF research effort was assigned to NASA in March 1967. The first aircraft (20207) made its 83rd, and final flight, to the Air Force Museum at Wright-Paterson AFB, Ohio, on 4 February 1969.

# NORTH AMERICAN (ROCKWELL) A-5 VIGILANTE

*North American (Rockwell) A-5 Vigilante of VAH-7 in the USS Enterprise. (Rockwell)*

**Type**: *Supersonic carrier-borne strike aircraft* **Crew**: *Two* **Manufacturers**: *North American Aviation, (Rockwell International), Columbus, Ohio* **Power Plant**: *Two 16,150 lb (7340 kg) st General Electric J79-2/-4 turbojets* **Dimensions**: *Span, 53 ft (16.15 m); Length, 75 ft 10 in (23.11 m); Height, 19 ft 5 in (5.92 m)* **Weights**: *Empty, 38,000 lb (17,240 kg); Loaded, 80,000 lb (36,285 kg)* **Performance**: *Max speed, 1,385 mph (2,230 km/h) (Mach 2.1); Service ceiling, 67,000 ft (20,400 m)*

The North American A3J-1 Vigilante was the last aircraft designed as a Mach 2 long-range strategic strike aircraft for carrier operation. In 1954 the US Navy had taken up the offer of a North American proposal for the NAGPAW (North American General-Purpose Attack Weapon) which called for an all-weather bomber capable of nuclear delivery using the new LABS (Low Altitude Bombing System).

The first YA3J-1 prototype flew for the first time on 31 August 1958 and deliveries to the US Navy began in August 1961. The A3J-1 (A-5A) was designed to carry either a Mk 27 nuclear weapon externally or a Mk 28 stored in an internal 'linear' bomb bay, from which the weapon could be ejected via a tunnel between the engine jet-pipes. Problems with the internal bay were never solved and it was subsequently used as a storage area for additional fuel tanks.

Only two Navy heavy attack squadrons were ever equipped with the Vigilante. With the cancellation of the US Navy's strategic nuclear strike role in 1962 in favour of the Polaris missile 59 early production A-5As and A-5Bs were converted to RA-5C multi-sensor reconnaissance aircraft. From 1964 former heavy attack squadrons were redesignated as RVAH (Reconnaissance Heavy Attack).

Some 109 Vigilantes were built during 1962-66 and 1969-71 and many reconnaissance variants served well in SE Asia. It remains one of the fastest, and heaviest, US Navy carrier-borne fighters.

# PANAVIA TORNADO

**Type**: *Multi-role combat aircraft. (ADV) Air Defence fighter* **Crew**: *Two* **Manufacturers**: *Panavia Aircraft GmbH, Munich, West Germany; British Aerospace (42 per cent); Messerschmitt-Bolkow-Blohm (42 per cent) and Aeritalia (15 per cent)* **Power plant**: *(IDS) Two 16,000 lb (7257 kg) reheat Turbo-Union (A consortium consisting of Rolls-Royce, MTU and Fiat) RB 199 34R Mk 101 turbo-fans. (ADV) Two RB 199 Mk 103/4 turbo-fans* **Dimensions**: *(IDS) Span, (max) 45 ft 8 in (13.90 m); Length, 54 ft 10¼ in (16.72 m); Height, 18 ft 8½ in (5.70 m). (ADV) Length, 58 ft 9 in (17.90 m)* **Weights**: *(IDS) Empty, 28,000 lb (12,700 kg); Loaded, 55,000 lb (25,000 kg). (ADV) Loaded, 52,000 lb (23,587 kg)* **Performance**: *Max speed, Mach 2.1* **Armament**: *(IDS)Two 27 mm IWKA-Mauser cannon with 125 rpg and various ordnance combinations on seven (three fixed and four swivelling) external stores stations. (ADV) one IKWA-Mauser cannon, four Skyflash air-to-air missiles under rear fuselage and up to four AIM-9 Sidewinder missiles*

On 26 March 1969 Aeritalia of Italy, Messerschmitt-Bölkow-Blohm (MBB) of West Germany and British Aircraft Corporation (now British Aerospace), combined to form a consortium, known as Panavia, to build the Tornado multi-role combat aircraft (MRCA). A total of 929 Tornadoes, consisting of the Interdiction and Strike (IDS), Air Defence Variant (ADV), and the Electronic Combat and Reconnaissance (ECR) variant, have been ordered by the three NATO nations.

The first prototype Tornado made its maiden flight from Manching in West Germany on 14 August 1974 and a further eight prototypes plus six pre-production aircraft had flown by 1981. On 1 July 1980 the first production aircraft were delivered to the Tri-National Tornado Training establishment at RAF Cottesmore. Formation of the first all-RAF Tornado unit began at RAF Honington at the end of June 1981 with the arrival of the first Tornadoes of the Tornado Weapons Conversion Unit (TWCU). The unit is designed to give

*Tornado F Mk 2 of No 65 Squadron (Shadow for 229 OCU).* (Author)

*Tornado GR Mk 1 of No 45 Squadron (Shadow for the TWCU - Tornado Weapons Conversion Unit) Honington, seen here taking off from RAF Marham in September 1986. (Author)*

each pilot 32 hours in-combat training after an initial course at the Tri-National Tornado Training establishment at Cottesmore. In December 1981 the Tornado GR Mk 1 made its operational debut in Exercise 'Mallet Blow'.

The GR Mk 1 first entered RAF service with No 9 Squadron at Honington on 9 June 1982. On 10 November 1982 one of the squadron's GR Mk 1s flew non-stop to Cyprus and back, a distance of 4,300 miles, refuelled in flight by Victor and Buccaneer tanker aircraft. No 9 Squadron's GR Mk 1s were followed into squadron service by 617 'Dambusters' Squadron at RAF Marham. In November 1984 Tornadoes from this squadron, supported by Victor tankers, participated in the US Strategic Air Command Bombing Competition, 'Giant Voice' at Ellsworth AFB, South Dakota. The 'Dambusters' took first and third place in the John C. Meyer Trophy, first and second in the Curtis LeMay Bombing Trophy and second and sixth place in the Mathis Trophy.

The Tornado GR Mk 1 has replaced Strike Command's Vulcans and Canberras in the UK. Beginning in February 1984, when 15 Squadron phased out its Buccaneers at Laarbruch, the Tornado had, by 1986, replaced all seven strike/attack squadrons of Buccaneers and Jaguars in RAF Germany. The Tornado GR Mk 1 is also destined to replace Strike Command Buccaneers in the early 1990s.

West Germany had on order 212 IDS versions for the Luftwaffe and 112 for the Marineflieger while 100 IDS versions have been built for the Aeronautica Militare Italiana. The total RAF order is for 229 IDS aircraft.

The ADV was designed specifically to meet RAF requirements for a long-range, all-weather interceptor and differs from the GR 1

*Tornado GR Mk 1 of No 27 Squadron on full power during a take-off from RAF Marham, September 1986.* (Author)

in having a longer forward fuselage to house AI-24 Foxhunter radar (in place of Decca Type 72 on the IDS version) and an extended rear fuselage to carry four Skyflash air-to-air missiles. Altogether, the RAF has on order 165 ADV aircraft.

The first 18 ADVs, which were fitted with RB 199 Mk 103 engines, and designated F Mk 2 were brought up to F Mk 3 standard and redesignated F Mk 2A while subsequent models, fitted with Mk 104 engines, are designated F Mk 3. This version has a number of improvements over the F Mk 2 including automatic wing sweep. The Tornado interceptor first flew on 27 October 1979 and entered service with No 229 OTU at Coningsby on 1 May 1985. The F Mk 3 entered operational service with No 5 Squadron which reformed from the Lightning at RAF Coningsby, Lincolnshire on 1 May 1988.

In 1986 the ECR version was chosen by the Luftwaffe and a total of 35 will be delivered from 1989 while the Italian Air Force has a requirement for 15 ECR Tornadoes. Foreign customers include Jordan, Oman and Saudi Arabia, which ordered 48 IDS and 24 ADV versions.

# SUPERMARINE S 5/S 6/S 6B

**Type**: *Racing seaplane* **Crew**: *Pilot only* **Manufacturers**: *Supermarine Aviation Works (Vickers) Ltd, Southampton* **Power Plant**: *(S 5) One 875 hp Napier Lion VIIB; (S 6) One 2,300 hp Rolls-Royce 'R'.* **Dimensions**: *(S 6) Span, 30 ft (9.14 m); Length, 28 ft 10 in (8.56 m); Height, 12 ft 3 in (3.75 m)* **Weights**: *Empty, 4,560 lb (2,072 kg); Loaded, 6,066 lb (2,757 kg);* **Performance**: *See text*

Seaplanes from five nations had competed in nine Schneider Trophy contests before the introduction of the Supermarine S 5 in the 1927 contest. The contest had been devised by Jacques Schneider, son of a French armaments owner and, appropriately, France was the first winner, in 1913. By 1922 Britain and Italy had each won the contest twice. Service teams dominated the next three contests, with US Navy pilots winning in 1923 and 1925 and Major Mario de Bernardi winning for Italy in 1926. Hubert Broad, who took second place in the 1925 contest in a Gloster IIIA, was the last civilian pilot to fly in the contests.

A military approach was the obvious answer and for the 1927 contest in Venice the RAF entered a team, made up of personnel from the RAF High Speed Flight, which had been formed in 1926, for the first time. Early in 1927 the Air Ministry ordered new racing seaplane designs from Glosters, Shorts and Supermarine. Three Gloster IVs and a Short Crusader were built. At Supermarine R.J. Mitchell produced the S 5, a development of the S 4 which had gained the world speed record on 13 September 1925 with a speed of 226.6 mph (364 km/h). The S 4 had a wooden fuselage and floats but the S 5 was of all-metal construction

with fabric covered, wire braced low wing and duralumin fuselage and floats. Power was provided by an 875 hp Napier Lion engine.

During the early summer of 1927 Flight-Lieutenant O.E. Worsley flew S 5, *N219* for the first time and in September this aircraft, accompanied by *N220* and the Gloster and Short seaplanes, were ferried to Italy aboard the carrier *Eagle*. On 26 September the three Italian Macchi M 52 monoplanes retired with mechanical problems and Flight-Lieutenant Sidney M. Webster won the contest with an average speed of 281.65 mph (453 km/h) in *N220*. Flight-Lieutenant Worsley came second in *N219* with an average speed of 273.07 mph (439 km/h). Flight-Lieutenant Webster also estab-

*The 1927 Schneider Trophy winning team with Reginald Mitchell (front row, centre) and Flight-Lieutenant N. Webster (top). The winning S 5 N220 was a geared version. The other aircraft which took part was N219, a direct drive version. (Vickers)*

lished a new world speed record over 100 kilometres with a speed of 283.66 mph (456 km/h). In 1928 Flight-Lieutenant D. D'Arcy Greig established a new British record in an S 5 with a speed of 319.57 mph (514 km/h).

Britain entered two Supermarine S 6 racing seaplanes, two Gloster VIs and the old S 5 N219 for the 1929 Schneider contest, which was held in September at Spithead. The bigger and heavier S 6 differed principally from the earlier S 5 in having a 1,900 hp Rolls Royce 'R' engine in place of the Napier Sabre. The Macchis were again plagued with mechanical problems and on 7 September Flying Officer H.R.D. Waghorn, in S 6 N247, won the trophy with an average speed of 328.63 mph (529 km/h). An M52R was second and the S 5 flown by Flight-Lieutenant D. D'Arcy Greig was placed third. Flying Officer R.L.R. Atcherley, in S 6 N248, established new world speed records of 332 and 331 mph (534/533

km/h) over 50 and 100 kilometres respectively. On 12 September Squadron Leader A.H. Orlebar AFC set a new world speed record of 357.7 mph (576 km/h) in S 6 N247.

A third successive win in the 1931 contest would give Britain outright victory and the right to keep the trophy for all time. Unfortunately, Marshal of the RAF Sir Hugh Trenchard did not consider the Schneider Trophy as a worthwhile investment and was opposed to the RAF's involvement. During 1930 the British Government refused to back the attempt on financial grounds and only relented when on 19 January 1931 Lady Lucy Houston promised a donation of £100,000 to ensure a British entry.

The High Speed Flight was reformed and with only eight months remaining, two of the 1929 S 6 seaplanes were fitted with larger floats and redesignated S 6A. Two new S 6B aircraft, S1595 and S1596, were built and the power of

the Rolls-Royce 'R' engine was increased to 2,300 hp. Fuel, oil and coolant systems were modified to meet the demands of the more powerful engine and the fuselage was strengthened.

The French, Italian and American entries withdrew from the 1931 contest and Britain was left to set new records. On 12 September Flight-Lieutenant J.N. Boothman in *S1595* set an average speed of 340.08 mph (547 km/h) to win the Coupe d'Aviation Maritime Trophy outright.

On 29 September Flight-Lieutenant G.H. Stainforth AFC established a new world speed record in S 6B *S1595* with a speed of 407.2 mph (654.90 km/h). The S 6B had become the first aircraft in the world to exceed 400 mph.

**Left** *Supermarine S 6B S1595, flown by Flight-Lieutenant J. N. Boothman in the 1931 Schneider Trophy Contest, won outright by Britain. In this aircraft Flight-Lieutenant G. H. Staniforth established a new world air speed record on 29 September 1931.* (Vickers)

**Below** *Supermarine S 6B S1596 of 1931.* (Vickers)

# SUPERMARINE SPITFIRE (Griffon-engined variants)

**Type**: *(XII, XIV, XVIII, XIX, Mk 21, 22 and 24) fighter* **Crew**: *Pilot only* **Manufacturers**: *Supermarine Division of Vickers-Armstrongs Ltd, Southampton, Swindon, Winchester and Castle Bromwich. Sub-contracted by Westland Aircraft and others* **Power Plant**: *(XII) Rolls-Royce Griffon III/IV. (XIV) Griffon 65. (XVIII) Griffon 65 or 67. (XIX) Griffon 65/66. (Mk 21,22,24) Griffon 61 or 85* **Dimensions**: *Span, 36 ft 10 in (11.23 m), (Clipped), 32 ft 2 in or 32 ft 7 in (9.93 m); Length, 32 ft 8 in (9.96 m); Height, 12 ft 9 in (3.89 m)* **Weights**: *(XIV) Empty, 6,700 lb (3040 kg); Loaded, 10,280 lb (4,663 kg)* **Performance**: *Max speeds: (XII) 393 mph (633 km/h) at 18,000 ft (5,490 m); (XIV) 448 mph (721 km/h) at 26,000 ft (7,930 m); (XVIII) 442 mph (712 km/h); (XIX) 460 mph (740 km/h); (F 21/F 22), 454 mph (730 km/h) at 26,000 ft (7,930 m)* **Armament**: *(XII/XIV), two 20 mm cannon and four .303 guns; 500 lb/1,000 lb of bombs. (XVIII) two 20 mm cannon, two .50 in guns and 1,000 lb of bombs. (XIX) None. (F 21/F 22) four 20mm cannon and 1,000 lb of bombs or rocket projectiles.*

The Spitfire was the most famous aircraft ever to see service with the RAF and was the only Allied fighter to remain in continuous production throughout the Second World War. In all, 27 different marks saw service up until 1947. In terms of speed the Griffon-engined versions were the most important Spitfires/Seafires produced.

During the Battle of Britain, Spitfires had gained a tactical advantage over Luftwaffe fighters. As the RAF turned to the offensive, Spitfire variants were developed to counter the threat posed by German fighters. The Spitfire V, fitted with a 1,440 hp Merlin 45 series engine, was developed to enable Fighter Command to retain its initiative over the Messerschmitt Bf 109 and the Spitfire IX, fitted with a 1,660 hp Merlin 61, was designed to meet the challenge posed by the Focke Wulf 190.

Early in 1943 there emerged the more powerful Rolls-Royce Griffon, which had a 36 per cent greater displacement than the Merlin, and was

capable of developing 1,735 hp at 1,000 feet. The RAF was anxious to get Griffon-engined Spitfires into action against low-flying FW 190 fighter-bombers which were making nuisance raids over the south coast of England almost at will. After trials involving a Spitfire III fitted with the Griffon IIB the Spitfire XII entered service with Nos 41 and 91 Squadrons at Hawkinge in the spring of 1943. Together with the Typhoon, the Griffon-engined Spitfire was an immediate success and was followed in production by the interim high-altitude Spitfire Mk XIV fitted with the 2,050 hp two-stage, two-speed supercharged Griffon 65 engine, driving a five-bladed propeller. The airframe was completely redesigned and the fin area increased to compensate for the longer nose.

The first of some 957 Spitfire XIVs built entered service with No 610 Squadron in January 1944. Operations against the V1 flying bomb began in June 1944 and ultimately Spitfire XIVs were responsible for the destruction of over 300 of these Doodlebugs. On 5 October 1944 a Spitfire XIV claimed the first Me 262 jet fighter to be destroyed by an Allied aircraft. On Christmas Eve three squadrons of Spitfire XIVs made the heaviest fighter-bomber attack of the war on V2 rocket sites on the Continent. Altogether, the XIV equipped some twenty squadrons in the 2nd Tactical Air Force and two in India shortly before the war's end.

The definitive wartime version of the Spitfire was the Mk XVIII F and FR version, which entered service just as the war ended. Prior to this model all Griffon-engined Spitfires had been interim versions, with the powerplant fitted into an existing airframe. The XVIII featured strengthened wings and undercarriage, extra fuel and a rear-view bubble hood, which had appeared on later production Mk XIVs, as standard. Altogether, 100 F XVIIIs and 200 FR XVIIIs were built. These were

**Above right** *Supermarine Spitfire F Mk XIIs of No 41 Squadron in starboard echelon. (IWM)*

**Right** *Spitfire Mk XIV at Kohima, 1945.*

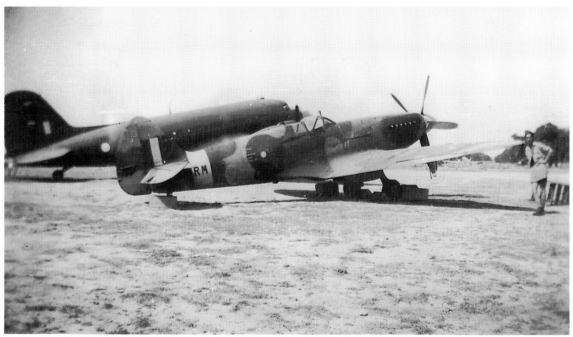

followed by 225 of the Mk XIX unarmed photo-reconnaissance version which was designed to replace the Spitfire XI in 1945. Fitted with the Griffon 65, the first twenty aircraft were unpressurised but the final 205 were fitted with the Griffon 66 and a pressure cabin together with increased wing tankage. The last RAF Spitfire sortie was made by Spitfire XIXs of No 81 Squadron in Malaya on 1 April 1954.

Other Griffon-engined Spitfires emerged post-war. Back in 1944 Supermarine had introduced a complete Spitfire redesign with higher tensile spar booms and a change in the planform. The redesign was too late for service in the Second World War but it emerged, with strengthened undercarriage and additional fuel tankage, as the F 21, 22 and 24 versions. A total of 121 F 21s were built before production switched to the F 22. It differed in having a rear-view bubble hood and cut down rear-fuselage. Later production F 22s were fitted with the Griffon 85 and contra-rotating pro-

**Above** *Spitfire F.22 fitted with contra-rotating airscrews.* (Vickers)

**Left** *Spitfire PR Mk XIX PS853, in photo reconnaissance blue, of the Battle of Britain Flight.* (Author)

pellers. A total of 278 F 22s were built and the majority served with the Royal Auxiliary Air Force from 1946–51.

The ultimate Spitfire design for the RAF was the F 24, which had a redesigned tail unit and was equipped with short barrel cannon and zero length rocket launchers. Only 54 had been built when deliveries ceased in October 1947, the majority being converted and uncompleted F 22 airframes. The F 24 saw service with No 80 Squadron in Germany and later Hong Kong, where it was finally replaced by the Hornet early in 1952.

Altogether, some 2,036 Griffon-engined Spitfires were built bringing the total Spitfire production for the RAF to 20,351.

# SUPERMARINE SWIFT 4

**Type**: *Interceptor fighter* **Crew**: *Pilot only* **Manufacturers**: *Supermarine Division of Vickers-Armstrongs Ltd, Winchester and Swindon* **Power Plant**: *(F.1) One 7,500 lb (3,409 kg) thrust Rolls-Royce Avon RA 7* **Dimensions**: *Span, 32 ft 4 in (9.87 m); Length, 41 ft 5½ in (12.66 m); Height, 12 ft 6 in (3.84 m)* **Performance**: *(FR 5) Max speed, 685 mph (1,103 km/h) at sea-level* **Armament**: *Two 30mm Aden cannon*

The Swift was ordered in November 1950 as a possible stand-in for the Hawker Hunter should this aircraft fail to meet expectations. Ironically, in Libya on 25 September 1953 the prototype Supermarine Swift 4, piloted by Lieutenant-Commander Michael Lithgow OBE, captured the world air speed record, previously held by the Hunter 3, with a speed of 735.70 mph (1,183.74 km/h). On 5 July it had flown from London to Paris in 19 minutes, 5.6 seconds at a speed of 669.3 mph (1,077.41 km/h).

The prototype Swift had flown for the first time on 5 August 1951 and a second, production standard, prototype made its maiden flight on 18 July 1952. A total of 150 Swifts were ordered for the RAF and four F 1s and the second prototype took part in the Coronation Review of 1953. No 56 Squadron began taking delivery of the F 1 in February 1954 but already there had been misgivings, particularly from the Americans during tests in 1952~53, about the long-term viability of an aircraft which had no aerodynamic advantage over the F-86 Sabre. The USAF pilots' criticism of the Swift's much higher wing loading, very poor controls and vicious wing drop, marked the beginning of the end for the Swift. Further criticism came

**Right** *The Swift established a number of records, including London to Paris in 19 minutes, 56 seconds at a speed of 669.3 mph (1,077.41 km/h) on 5 July 1953.* (Vickers)

**Below** *The Swift F 4 prototype, with Lieutenant-Commander Mike Lithgow at the controls, taxies in after setting a new air speed record in Libya on 25 September 1953.* (Vickers)

from the Central Fighter Establishment at West Raynham and the Aircraft and Armament Experimental Establishment at Boscombe Down.

Only 36 Swift F 1/2s were built and the aircraft was withdrawn from Fighter Command in May 1955, future F 5 models being used solely for fighter-reconnaissance. Although it equipped only one squadron as an interceptor the Swift nevertheless established a number of speed records and was the first swept-wing fighter to enter service with the RAF.

# SPACE SHUTTLE

**Type**: *Aerospacecraft* **Crew**: *Five-seven* **Manufacturers**: *Rockwell International* **Power Plant**: *Three rocket engines each of 375,000 lb (170,454 kg) thrust at sea level. Rocket boosters: 2,900,000 lb (13,166,000 kg) thrust each at sea level.* **Dimensions**: *Span, 78.06 ft (23.79 m). Length, 122.2 ft (37.25 m)* **Weight**: *150,000 lb (68,100 kg)* **Performance**: *See text*

The USA's attempt to put astronauts into space aboard a re-usable spacecraft, has, since 1972, cost $9900 million. The Space Shuttle has been built to fly scientists into orbit for 7-30 days, launch satellites and space probes and to be used to rescue astronauts who may be stranded in orbit or retrieve and repair satellites which have failed.

The Shuttle is composed of a delta-wing orbiter, a 154 foot long external liquid fuel tank and two re-usable solid rocket boosters which are jettisoned into the ocean from a height of 28 miles. Although the fuel tank is also jettisoned into the ocean it is not retrieved. Each Shuttle is designed to fly a minimum of 100 missions and can withstand temperatures of up to 3,000°F during re-entry. The Shuttle's cargo bay is 60 feet long and 15 feet in diameter and can carry up to 65,000 lb (29,545 kg) into orbit. The payloads will eventually include a manned orbital laboratory (Spacelab), satellites and spacecraft. It can return 32,000 lb (14,545 kg) of payload to earth.

The first launch took place on 12 April 1981 when the Space Shuttle Orbiter 'Columbia', commanded by Commander John W. Young USN and piloted by Robert L. Crippen, blasted off from Cape Canaveral, Florida. (Young was the Apollo astronaut who walked on the Moon in April 1972). 'Columbia' broke all records for

**Above right** *Space Shuttle Discovery touches down at Edwards AFB, California, on 3 September 1985 after a successful space mission in which three satellites were launched and one recovered and repaired before being redeployed into space again.* (NASA)

**Right** *Space Shuttle atop a Boeing 727 during its flight from the Paris Air Show to Stansted in June 1983.* (Author)

*The Space Shuttle is proudly displayed at Stansted Airport in June 1983.* (Author)

space flight by a fixed wing craft with a speed of 16,600 mph (26,715 km/h) at main engine cut-off. 'Columbia' completed re-entry to the earth's atmosphere from 400,000 feet (122,000 m) and landed at Rogers Dry Lake at Edwards AFB, Southern California on 14 April 1981.

'Columbia' has also set an absolute world record for duration of 8 days, 4 minutes, 45 seconds with two astronauts. The Space Shuttle 'Challenger', which was launched on 18 June 1983, set a duration record of 6 days, 2 hours, 23 minutes and 59 seconds with five astronauts. On an earlier mission 'Columbia' set a new world altitude record of 206.36 miles (332.1 km).

The Space Shuttle 'Discovery' with a five-man crew led by Commander Joe H. Engle and including pilot Richard O. Covey, was launched in September 1985. It touched down at Edwards AFB on 3 September after a mission in which three satellites were launched and a satellite launched earlier in the year was retrieved from space, repaired and redeployed into space.

The Space Shuttle 'Challenger' was destroyed soon after launch from Cape Canaveral on 28 January 1986, killing all seven (five men and two women) crew.

# WORLD AIR SPEED RECORDS 1929~90

| Date | Pilot | Aircraft | Speed (mph) |
|---|---|---|---|
| 12 Sept 1929 | Sqdn Ldr A. H. Orlebar | Supermarine S 6 | 357.75 |
| 29 Sept 1931 | Flt Lt G. H. Staniforth | Supermarine S 6B | 407.02 |
| 3 Sept 1932 | James Doolittle | Gee Bee R-1 | †296.28 |
| 4 Sept 1933 | Jimmy Wedell | Wedell-Williams | †305.33 |
| 4 Sept 1934 | Raymond Delmotte | Caudron C 460 | †314.3 |
| 10 Apr 1934 | W/O Francesco Agello | Maachi MC 72 | 423.85 |
| 23 Oct 1934 | Lt Francesco Agello | Maachi MC 72 | 440.69 |
| 13 Sept 1935 | Howard Hughes | Hughes H-1 | †352.4 |
| 30 Mar 1939 | Flug Kapt Hans Dieterle | Heinkel He100V-8 | 463.92 |
| 26 Apr 1939 | Flug Kapt Fritz Wendel | Bf 209V | 469.22 |
| 7 Nov 1945 | Gp Capt H. J. Wilson | Gloster Meteor IV | 606.38 |
| 7 Sept 1946 | Gp Capt E. M. Donaldson | Gloster Meteor IV | 615.78 |
| 19 June 1947 | Col Albert Boyd | Lockheed P-80R | 623.74 |
| 20 Aug 1947 | Cdr Turner Caldwell | Douglas D-558-I | 640.74 |
| 25 Aug 1947 | Maj Marion E. Carl | Douglas D-558-I | 650.92 |
| 15 Sept 1948 | Maj Richard L. Johnson | F-86A Sabre | 670.98 |
| 19 Nov 1952 | Capt Slade J. Nash | F-86D Sabre | 698.50 |
| 16 July 1953 | Lt Col William Barnes | F-86D Sabre | 715.75 |
| 7 Sept 1953 | Sqdn Ldr Neville Duke | Hawker Hunter 3 | 727.63 |
| 25 Sept 1953 | Lt Cdr Mike Lithgow | Supermarine Swift | 735.70 |
| 3 Oct 1953 | Lt Cdr James B. Verdin | XF4D-I Skyray | 752.94 |
| 29 Oct 1953 | Lt Col Frank K. Everest | YF-100 Super Sabre | 755.15 |
| 20 Aug 1955 | Col H. A. Hanes | F-100C Super Sabre | 822.27 |
| 10 Mar 1956 | Peter Twiss | Fairey Delta FD 2 | 1132.00 |
| 12 Dec 1957 | Maj Adrian Drew | F-101A Voodoo | 1207.60 |
| 16 May 1958 | Capt Walter Irvin | Lockheed F-104A | 1404.09 |
| 31 Oct 1959 | Col Georgiy Mosolov | Sukhoi E-66 | 1483.83 |
| 15 Dec 1959 | Maj Joseph W. Rogers | F-106A Delta Dart | 1525.95 |
| 22 Nov 1961 | Lt Col Robert Robinson | McDonnell F4H-1F | 1606.51 |
| 7 Jul 1962 | Col Georgiy Mosolov | Sukhoi Type E-166 | 1665.89 |
| 1 May 1965 | Col Robert L. Stephens | Lockheed Yf-12A | 2070.10 |
| Aug 1966 | Mike Carroll | Hawker Sea Fury | *520.00 |
| 28 July 1976 | Capt Eldon W. Joersz | Lockheed SR-71A | 2193.16 |
| April 1981 | Robert L. Crippen | Space Shuttle | 16,600.00 |

\* Piston-engined record. † Landplane record

### Progressive Air-Launched Record

| | | | |
|---|---|---|---|
| 2 Oct 1941 | Heini Dittmar | Bf 163 Komet | 623.00 |
| 14 Oct 1947 | Captain Charles Yeager | Bell X-1 | 700.00 |
| Nov 1953 | Scott Crossfield | D-558-II Skyrocket | 1327.00 |
| 12 Dec 1953 | Capt Charles Yeager | Bell X-1A | 1612.00 |
| 27 Sept 1956 | Capt Milburn Apt | Bell X-2 | 2094.00 |
| 3 Oct 1967 | W. J. Knight | X-15A-2 | 4534.00 |

# INDEX